ENLIGHTENMENT

ENLIGHTENMENT

Revelations from the Higher Realm

Through Rev. Robert E. Wagner

Narrated by Cha Lea

Order this book online at www.trafford.com
or email orders@trafford.com

Most Trafford titles are also available at major online book retailers.

Printed in the United States of America.

ISBN: 978-1-4669-0637-2 (sc)
ISBN: 978-1-4669-0638-9 (e)

Trafford rev. 01/11/2012

 www.trafford.com

North America & international
toll-free: 1 888 232 4444 (USA & Canada)
phone: 250 383 6864 ✦ fax: 812 355 4082

Table of Contents

Part I

Part II

Information given to Mankind from the White Brotherhood
through Melchizedek, a High Priest to God,

Through Rev. Robert E. Wagner

Narrated by Cha Lea

Forward

You know the song—"Is that all there is?" Is what we see, hear, feel, taste and smell all there is? The answer to that question is NO! There is a whole other realm for mankind to access or tap into. The Spiritual Realm!

Mankind has reached a point in his existence where they are dissatisfied with the status quo. The world unrest; wars, famine, disease, cut throat competition, etc. are all a part of this unrest.

There is every indication, at this time in our history, that we must find a different way; a different path to our destiny.

We look around us and try to compare our life's circumstances; job, home, friends, and opportunities and by doing so we are setting ourselves up for dissatisfaction and disappointment because there will always be someone with greater and or lesser opportunities than ourselves. This condition is sometimes carried so far as to cause war or in lesser degrees, to cause dissatisfaction and brutal competition and dis-ease which when connected—is disease!

This book was written for the purpose of finding a path to the spiritual side of our being; to admit to, to recognize and to tap into that realm where we can find peace, happiness and true love from our Creator: God our Father; and for our fellow man.

That realm is the only reality there is. We come from the Spiritual Realm to be of service to our creator by connecting with Him; listening for His guidance and applying His wisdom to the people for the betterment and growth of mankind. First you have to recognize that He is there for our guidance and His love. Then we must learn how to tap into His realm through meditation and prayer. This can be done. The desire on our part must be vast, sincere and serious enough for God to reach us and touch our souls.

Prayer is talking to God; Meditation is listening to God . . . listening for His help and guidance in answering our prayers. You will not hear His answer in words necessarily, but you will have thoughts, feelings, impressions and at times, road blocks will be put in your way to keep you from getting in harms way.

As it says in the first dissertation from the higher realm, your body is the vehicle your spirit uses to travel in while you are on the earth plane. The real you is spirit. God is spirit . . . you are spirit. It is through your spirit that you have the ability to contact God.

Your spirit is the part of you that is connected to the Spiritual Realm; where all the life giving forces are available and ready to be tapped by man when he is ready to admit that what he tries to do under his own steam is not enough and he finally humbles himself enough to go to God for the answers he needs for any and all situations he finds himself in.

The information given to mankind in this book is for the soul purpose of enlightening mankind of the relationship between Him, us and the Higher Realm.

We are here on earth to act as emissaries of God, to carry out His plan for the good of His people.

As you absorb or understand this information and allow yourself to be a channel; an avenue through which the great God Force can flow, there will be no limit as to what you can accomplish for you and your fellowman.

Christis Spirit

———

THE CHRIST SPIRIT is the controlling force of your sphere of influence. He—if you want to use this vernacular—is not a God, but a force. He is a symphony. He is a complete spiritual body. He is the motivating force behind all activity on this plane of existence

The reason we use the word body, is to cause you to associate the complexity of this great force in a manner in which you can visualize. The Christ Spirit has no form.

The Christ Spirit also has a greater force and there are greater forces than these again. You must be aware of the fact that the force . . . the great intelligence which controls the movements of great bodies as well as the movements of the finest of living mechanisms, must have intelligence greater than it, which is capable of perfecting complete balance of elements of life.

Now, these forces are available to all under proper conditions. When one has attained a level of intelligence capable of absorbing the harmonics at the higher vibratory rate, they can accomplish great influential positions in your plane of existence. Now, this repeats itself in other universes of which there are countless numbers of universes . . . staggering beyond your capability of comprehension. Each of these has an equivalent of your Christ Spirit. The Christ Spirit manifests basically through the one you call Melchizedek. Many referred to him as Father, Jesus of Nazareth spoke of him as the Father, the source closest to the ultimate, God.

Melchizedek is one step from the Christ Spirit . . .

This book constitutes a series of lectures given through Reverend Robert E. Wagner via contact of the Spirits of Melchizedek, Jeremiah, Zechariah and other priests and prophets for the good of mankind.

So that the revelations received from the Higher Spirit Realm may be more readily assimilated by mankind, these lectures have been narrated in this book verbatim from the original transcripts dictated through The Reverend Robert E. Wagner while in deep meditation.

For there is nothing covered that shall not be revealed; neither hidden, that shall not be known.

Therefore, whatever ye have spoken in darkness shall be heard in the light; and that which ye have spoken in the ear in private rooms shall be proclaimed upon the housetops.

Luke 12: 2,3

Part 1

Chapter 1

Search For Truth

THERE ARE THOSE who have an intense desire to believe in something. They are looking for inspiration outside themselves. They are looking for a stimulus or a force to take over and overwhelm them. In this way they would know that there is great power available to them. Now this is a common conception amongst man. Man, in general, looks to others for his guidance and he looks to blame others for his failures This is normal, for instinctively man attempts to hold himself blameless in all situations. This, if one wants to succeed in the world, must be overcome, for this tendency does not strengthen one but weakens the individual. When one considers outside influences, then one admits to himself that these outside influences are greater than he. He admits that the men and women surrounding him are greater than he, but conversely he tends to tear their characters down to build his ego up. He is instinctively trying to justify his failures in others.

One normally, is most critical of his own weaknesses and of those around and about him when he witnesses them. He becomes annoyed by these weaknesses. This is what we call evil. Evil and ignorance are synonymous to our way of thinking. When you are told by the Master Teacher (Spirit is talking about Jesus as the Master Teacher), that you were born in sin and that when you are enlightened you are free from sin, most people felt that He was talking about crime, as you call it, but crime and sin are not synonymous. Crime is the result of sin and when your are enlightened you no longer see life from a materialistic point of view and you throw off the mental images which prevail with materialistic points of view.

So sin is being born with the lack of knowledge of what is real and what is not real. When you are young and your sense of taste, of touch, of smell and of sight develop early your sensations are transferred to your mind through these human devices acquainting you with the new expressions which you find yourself exposed to. Now if you approach life, as you call it, attempting to satisfy the feelings created by your five material senses, you are living in ignorance and evil. When you mature, your materialistic urges for satisfaction of taste and touch tend to diminish and you begin to realize that there is something beyond the sensations, the thrills of material existence. You find yourself dissatisfied with these indulgences and you start to examine what is apparently real and what is not real.

Your physical body is a manifestation of the mental image created by you to carry out your mission in life. It is a mental image vibration at a lower plane of vibration than your spiritual plane of vibration. So your spiritual realm is reality. The thought that causes our action is the activating element and the action itself is a response to that thought. It makes no difference what device is used to cause a thought to manifest itself and at spirit level we care not whether this thought is transferred through what you call a male or female. At this plane of existence, we place no greater importance on entities which tend to one pattern of thought than another, for we have found that there are many mansions or categories of thought in the Christ consciousness just like there are many branches, leaves and roots to make up a tree. It takes many facets of existence to make up a spirit complex or body.

Each of you is a part of a spiritual body and each of you performs a function to benefit the body as a whole, Just as each cell in your body performs it's function to benefit the material body, each entity performs it's function to benefit the overall spirit body and they are all interdependent. You are part of the great force and you are guided by spirit to be joined in unison to assist in performing the great tasks of the great force. So it behooves us to have each of you perform your duties to the best of your abilities. For no chain is stronger than it's weakest link.

That is why we are so concerned and make a diligent effort to segregate entities from a group and attract others to the same group, for there must be a compatibility and a mutuality amongst the spirit entities, to work in harmony with one another and in this way the individual finds himself content and at ease in his surroundings. When the individual is content and at ease, it becomes rather difficult to disturb; to irritate; to rile this individual. When one feels at ease with those around and about him, one drops fear and anxiety and replaces them with deep love for fellow man and countenance.

Those who sincerely desire to become in tune with this great sphere of influence, will prosper and those who seek self glory will flounder by the wayside. It has been said that man cannot live by bread alone, You will sit by the Master Teacher and wish to be fulfilled but the water you drink of this dipper is not fulfilling. You must struggle to gain this state of existence you are seeking and when your desire is great enough, you will find yourself by losing yourself in this great force. This is important to remember; in order to obtain greatness and recognition, one must seek humbleness; one must lose themselves completely in their mission and in the process of allowing their mission to be accomplished through them they will attain greatness.

Of what use is a finger that does not have the palm of the hand? Of what use is an eye that does not have the nerve to transfer the thought of the image to the mind? The palm of your hand will do it's best to feed the finger all the energy; all the impulses to have that finger perform it's duties well.

Now the average artist is considered eccentric. Many people could well learn the lesson that an artist has learned early in childhood, for an artist has learned to tune into a realm beyond the touch of average materialistic thinking. An artist will give of himself to the great inspiring force and will record what he sees or hears to the best of his ability. This artist loses himself in the mission and the more he gives of himself to this great force the more beautiful; the more moving his work becomes and the works are what you judge the artist by. You do not judge him by his appearance or his manner of living, for these are soon forgotten. You judge the artist's greatness by his works.

You judge a teacher not by what he says nor by the way he dresses but by his ability to inspire in his student the desire to develop to his full potential. The more he loses himself in the needs of his students and humbles himself to their needs and forgets himself, the greater inspiration is transferred to his students.

AND YE SHALL KNOW THE TRUTH AND THE TRUTH SHALL MAKE YOU FREE. (John8:32). Truth is so simple; the requirements are so simple that they are not believed by the average entity on your plane of existence. They feel that life, of necessity, must be quite complicated; quite involved and this is incorrect. Life is quite simple when you know that you have available to you at all times all the forces, any one of which you can use at any given time merely by tuning in to spirit and giving of yourself as an instrument through which this great power or force can express itself.

Chapter 2

Motivation

IF THERE IS one who aspires to great wealth, he can have great wealth but if he is attempting to gain his great wealth by intrigue and at the expense of those around and about him, he will never attain it.

It is quite common for a person who is evil, to feel that to amass great wealth, one must be devious and cunning in their activities towards their fellowman. Like the man who paints a great picture or composes great music; the man who causes his fellowman to be inspired to work for a common goal receives his reward. If you wish to be a millionaire you must think as a millionaire thinks. You must be humble. You show me a great man in industry and I will show you a man who prays, for the greater a man becomes the fewer people he can consult with on the material plane. Therefore, he looks to the unseen for his inspiration, ideas and creations which are usually contrary to most materialistic thinking.

Fortunes are created they are not earned. Fortunes are the result of creative thought and one's ability to lose himself in bringing these visions and creations to fulfillment. If you wish to be wealthy by material means, set aside your material desire for obtaining great wealth and put first things first. Open your hearts and your minds to great spiritual inspiration and receive this inspiration and transpose it into action, continually seeking spiritual guidance so that you do not stray from the original intent of this vision, inspiration, hunch or ideal and you will attract those who are required by you to bring about the fruition of this idea or inspiration. BUT SEEK YE FIRST THE KINGDOM OF GOD AND HIS RIGHTEOUSNESS, AND ALL THESE THINGS SHALL BE ADDED UNTO YOU. (Matthew 6: 33)

You are the creator of your idea and as a result of your creation, your fellowman reimburses you, generally in excess of what you would normally accept or expect. So, it behooves you at all times to examine the motive for your actions, for this is the key to health, happiness, and prosperity.

The motivating force behind all action is the key. When you allow ego and pride to influence your thought patterns, you deviate from this image; you deviate from this vision and it becomes imperfect. You cease to inspire those around and about you and you wonder why. They, by instinct, know that you are not pure in your thinking and they suspect your motive and abandon you or if they work with you, they work with reservation and suspicion and you are subject to bringing about an imperfect performance. You feel frustrated and ill at ease and this is a corresponding disharmony within your thought pattern. This thought pattern distorts your spirit body and if your spirit body is not perfect, your material reflection will show this imperfection. And if you hold this disharmonious thought for any length of time, you create a permanent distortion in your physical manifestation of your thought pattern; you may call this an illness if you wish.

Illness is a habit of an erroneous conception of yourself and your relationship with those around and about you. You must correct this image, for in correcting an image, you must also correct your motives, for all life is generated from motive. Your reason for performing an act is what you are judged by not the act itself. What was your intent? When we find someone who will open themselves to us (Spirit) and unfortunately there is such a small percentage of those who will; we indulge them completely, and they are the ones you commemorate, whose company you desire to be in and who inspire you to great tasks, that is, to work beyond their normal capabilities. Your normal capabilities are as great as theirs except that you have created a mental image of your limitations. You tell yourself that you cannot do these things. The man who does these things knows no fear. He knows he is going to have problems but he knows no fear for he knows that as fast as these problems come up he has those around and about him who will assist him in overcoming his obstacles in order to bring about his mission. He has faith in his ability to contact spirit and ability within himself. He has faith in his ability to contact spirit and have his answers at will.

Faith, motive and humbleness are the ingredients of greatness and recognition. The combination of these three things is the key to success in any endeavor. It makes no difference what your chosen field; that is incidental. There is no field that is of greater importance than any other field of expression, so that if you apply these rules to any field you find yourself involved in, you will have equal success; equal recognition and equal reward for your humbleness.

Every great man, if you read biographies, at one time or another, has been exposed to a great defeat and at that time he humbles himself and realizes the futility of materialistic thinking. Then and only then does he start to rise to greatness.

Chapter 3

─────

Aura

YOUR AURA, AS you call it, appears to us as a street light having a white center from which radiates a spectrum. You control the color of your aura by your thought process. Each individual has a normal core color, and each individual thought you have shows up in a fluctuating aura around the center core color. It is this fluctuating color combination which transmits your thought to us and we in turn will be attracted to these and will transmit our thoughts through this aura to the core and to the inner light or the real you. Then you, in turn, transfer this thought image or impression to your material expression, This is basically, in simple terms, our means of contact.

Each thought, basically, will give a burst of color and this indicates to us the manner of thinking of the individual emitting this energy. Your spirit light will vary in intensity and proportion to the strength of your desire. The greater your desire the greater the intensity of light. This light, generally, is white. However, you

─────

may find it in a field of blue, orange, purple, or it may be in the full spectrum.

You will find that when a group of people sit and meditate together regularly, they will tend to a common desire and consequently have a constant coloring forming a band of great intensity. You appear to us then, as certain combinations of stars in the heavens and we look for these concentrations and favor them with our attention. This is also true for healing, for as you obtain proper attitudes for healing, your core color takes on a similar hue of violet that emits jointly. And do not have any doubts, for even though each individual has a different avenue of expression of our great love force, each of you is important to us; each of you will serve and is serving in a manner which is important to us. It is the flow of the love force which heals. The greater your trust, the stronger your desire the better instrument you become; the more intense your light; the more vast the circle of your core becomes and the more area we have to contact you.

Therefore, your force will increase in proportion to the size of the core of your desires. This will explain to you why you will increase your proficiency as time goes on, but we will not allow this love force to be abused for any length of time. There are those who would glorify themselves in being instruments of these great forces who will ascend to great heights rapidly and like a comet or meteor, burn out and disintegrate rapidly and that which glorified them will ultimately disillusion them, for they have abused the basic law. But those who lose themselves in the great forces will forever grow and grow performing greater works upon greater works. This is as it is and ever will be.

The only controlling factor is your faith in and your ability to contact these forces. Do not assume that there are magic words to invoke a particular force for there are none. You trigger any given force or you attract any given force to you by your intense desire to use this force for the benefit of those around and about you. This is the only means of positive contact. There are lesser forces operating at a lower plane of existence which may be tapped by those who wish to use others and express themselves through others for selfish means but the strength of these forces is quite limited. These lesser forces are available but once you have been in contact with higher forces, you build a shield around yourself which the lower forces cannot penetrate and this should relieve you of fear. Like attracts like and if you contact the lower spirits you will get lower entities and that is not good.

The lower level of contact may be entertaining at times but never of great magnitude. There are many who tap this lower level and glorify themselves and suddenly find themselves being stymied by their limitations. Then there are those at the lower level who have not given up their enjoyment of using others and abusing others for their own entertainment and you see the results in the lower level of medium ship. The motivating thought or prayer, depending on the intensity of your desire, determines the level of contact.

Chapter 4

Spirit Contact

THERE ARE MANY names for the physical manifestation which you call your body. Some call it your temple. It is your individual temple that was provided for you to worship in. It is your physical means to manifest your thoughts and visualizations which are given to you.

You must understand that if you are spirit; and your spirit and our spirit are not unlike one another; then it is logical that you should be able to transfer your thoughts and visions to us and likewise we could do the same. You must understand that this spirit that dwells within your temple is the point of focus; the point of contact which we use in manifesting ourselves to you.

This spark of life, as you call it, is you and this spark of life is infinitesimally small but it is there. If you wish to meditate and contact us, it would be well to understand that your means of contact is through this tiny light. If you wish to contact the higher realm, you look inwardly to seek out this tiny light and focus on it. You have the power within you to change the color and the intensity of this tiny light and it will magnify itself and we will be able to distinguish you from other lights.

And when you magnify yourself, you become brighter, more intense and greater in volume so that we can contact you more readily, for as your light intensifies, you raise your vibration and when you have transcended the first two planes of existence above the so called material plane we can contact you more easily.

You need not give of yourself completely to us to have us speak to you; it is not necessary. Darkness is not necessary for meditation. The only condition that is necessary, is your intense desire to contact us. However, to receive manifestations, it is important that the room be totally devoid of artificial light. Spirit cannot manifest as long as there is light in the room.

When you put yourself into a prayerful state and lose consciousness of your physical self and are alert to what we wish to give you in thought or vision you will find yourself rewarded. We are constantly alert to those on your plane who are desirous of giving of themselves to the needs of those around and about them. And when we see this earnest desire, we respond immediately. We do not hesitate for we are alert; we are ever alert, so it is to your benefit to have a firm undiluted desire or prayer, if you want to call it that. Concentrate deeply and thoroughly without any doubts and you will make instantaneous contact.

You can, at will, tap any force at any given moment depending upon the need for this force. You are an individual who has complete freedom of choice at any given time as to what band or which force you are tapping to accomplish the desired results. These bands or forces are here at all times and are available at all times. Therefore, you must have a clear undiluted desire that is directed to the force which you wish to tap at any given moment. Then combine yourself with this force. This is the most difficult level of attainment. Everyone, instinctively, resists losing oneself in the great force and this is unfortunate for to lose yourself in this great force is to find yourself

Lose yourself within this great force and you have no limitations; you have no fear. We do not wish to consume you. We wish to expand you and we also wish to expand our influence. This is why we would not dare to consume one who is giving us an avenue of expression, whether it be knowledge of healing, of wisdom, or of understanding, for there are many forces here.

The fear of losing your identity is a basic fear. You feel as though you may be a drop of water being lost in a stream going to sea. This is fear and fear is of the devil. Fear and it's derivatives are basically the cause of all dissension and illness in man. If you were but to tune in and bathe yourself in the intelligence of these great powers that are available to you at any given moment, there would be no problem too great to solve; no problem greater than the intelligence of the great force. No individual light on the earth plane is greater than the force. It cannot and never shall be.

If you wish to do great works, you must have great desires and you must be consistent in these great desires. Then you will be accepted in this great band and spirit will work through you readily. Your works will be great by man's standards but not by our standards. To us, what you call great works are the normal ways to us. It is important that you examine your motives, for the intensity and the purity of your motives is what generates your light. The purer your light, the stronger the contact of the great force. Do not idly toy with contact to the spirit world but intensify your desires. Humble yourself to the point where you become part of a force and allow a force to become part of you and flow through you and we will perform great works through you. This will cause you to become exceptional in your abilities and your rewards will be great, for your abilities will be exceptional as compared to the standards of your fellowman and all your material needs will be more than adequately cared for.

Each individual is capable of contacting the higher realm, through proper meditation and of receiving instruction or messages, as you call them, directly from the higher realm. We strongly discourage individuals from giving messages, as a medium, for those around and about them. We wish to encourage complete trance conditions only for giving messages. When conditions are correct and man has overcome his anxiousness to demonstrate his ability to contact spirit, we will contact man to give advice to others through a medium of our choice only. No one is to give a message unless we inform them that this message is urgent for the party involved. This is the true intent of medium—ship. We would normally prefer to speak to the individual directly but only in an emergency do we intend to invoke these thoughts on one who is in the presence because of conditions beyond the control of the recipient.

Each of you has had what you call a hunch; each of you has heard voices; each of you have seen visions. But only in a condition of complete relaxation or moments when you do not expect it does it happen properly. This is as we wish it and this is as it will be in the not too distant future, We will choose, as we have in the past, our teachers, as there are not many which we speak directly to. There will not be many chosen as teachers as there are not many who are willing to place the contact with the higher realm ahead of their material ambitions. Consequently, teachers are few.

Chapter 5

Healing Forces

THERE IS SOME concern as to the validity and availability of the great healing force and the ways and means of utilizing this great force, not only to help those around and about you but also to cleanse yourself of your own infirmities. You say to yourself, "if there is such a force available, why is there so much illness?"

You are born in ignorance of the law, and as you violate the law in ignorance, you create images in your physical and your thought patterns which are then reflected in your individual expressions and you create conditions within yourself that are undesirable. This great force is available to you but it seems as though until an entity comes to the brink of disaster he doesn't trouble himself to find himself. Then when he does find out what he is made of he investigates and finds out that he is spirit first and that his flesh is but a manifestation or solidified visualization of himself. This temple which you walk around in is a result of your thought patterns. You are a small spark in a vast sea of ectoplasm and you have placed a barrier around you which does not allow this great spirit force to penetrate. This is due to your material so-called urge of self preservation.

Let's say you build yourself a glove in which you live and in order for us to flow to you and through you, you must break down this imaginary barrier you have created and allow this great force to penetrate.

This great force is like an oasis in the desert. You must struggle to get to this oasis and as you struggle to attain this oasis you cleanse yourself of all importance of material gain. When you have the desire for this water of life, you suddenly realize the futility of all indulgences and seek the water of life; losing yourself in this desire. In the process of losing yourself in this desire you find yourself; you find the real you; you find the relative importance of that which surrounds you and you realize that your spirit and your ethereal body, as you call it, are the only reality. The rest is conjured up by your lower level of thinking.

This great healing force then, is available. It flows freely through the individual to other individuals just like sound traveling through water and is transferred to yet other individuals and goes on and on. The farther away from the source the lesser the vibration; the lesser the impact. The slower the value of the tone, the slower and weaker the vibration. It is like that in reality, for as one attains higher vibrations they attract higher vibrations. Any thought that the 'Great I Am' sends down becomes lesser and lesser in vibration and unfortunately, great thoughts are dissipated at this plane of existence because we are unable to find those who have attained a high enough vibration or desire to receive these thoughts to transfer them to mankind.

It behooves every individual to raise their vibration to intensify their desire and faith so that they may receive these great thoughts and have mankind and those around the individual also benefit by these great thoughts. These great forces are available to you but you must have faith; you must have intense desire and you must lose yourself in what you wish to accomplish. Then you will have tapped into the great force that is available to you and your rewards will be great.

If you would but realize that your desires control your ability to utilize the forces which are available to you. We recognize your motives. Your motives are the triggering force. The strength of your motivation generates the power within you which raises your vibratory level to a level that we can sense. We then are attracted to this vibration which you emit, for when we get within your realm we sense your motives and we respond accordingly.

Envision yourself not as being a force within yourself, as so many of you tend to think thus creating an erroneous thought within your being, but rather be satisfied with being a directing force for the power which is available to you, for your limits of attainment are limitless. We need a motivating beam of concentration of thought to solidify our reactions to your thought pattern and the greater the beam or light, the greater the effect you will have and the greater the work that can be accomplished by the force which is directed by you.

The only reality in existence is thought. You are the result of your thought patterns, or as you call them, habits. You have, as individuals, great potential but as individuals, you unfortunately look to yourselves for the abilities and limit yourselves to the capabilities that are generated within you as an individual and consequently find your works mediocre. Once you have been overwhelmed by the light of what you call the Christ Spirit, you desire to be bathed in this light from time to time and in order to be bathed in this light, you must have an extremely strong desire not to be bathed in the light but to use this light for the benefit of those around and about you. Once you learn this simple truth, you will have disintegrated the shell that has been placed around you and there will be no bounds for the work that can be performed by you. Remember, you are the focusing force that is the vibrating beam or if you wish, the radio signal; you set the wave length and we tune in to augment it.

Elaborate on your desire. A moment of intense desire is far more effective than just wishing to have something happen. It is the intensity, the undiluted thought that invokes this great power. We do not ask you to do the work but you must cleanse yourself of thoughts of distrust; thoughts of awareness or of limitations, for you are merely a vehicle through which this great force can flow.

Remember, when you are standing about a person whom you wish to have adjusted or healed, you are controlling the waves of energy. You merely request that we examine a being and cause to flow through you, the proper harmonic element which will overcome and provide what is needed for this person. You are a vehicle and the more you use your healing ability the more you individually gain by clarifying your own harmonics within your individual system. Remember this well because this is the area of expression of Jesus of Nazareth.

In order to perform healings, it is necessary that your physical condition be chemically proper. To become sensitive to the vibrations of the one before you to be healed, you must have eliminated from your own system, the chemicals which tend to slow down your vibratory rate. Any fluid or food which has a sedentary effect, affects your ability to transfer the healing force. Therefore any compound which contains caffeine is detrimental to your system. You must cultivate the habit of drinking juices of fruit and vegetables. The water you drink is desirable but it is not preferable. High sugar content foods are quite detrimental to your system. You will note that when you eat foods with high starch or sugar content there is a brief and only a brief period of acceleration followed by a long period of feeling logy or sometimes a minor state of depression.

These things cause a sedentary effect on the system and clog the nervous system as well as the fuel system. One is as detrimental as the other. This is why a person who is highly nervous will snack constantly for they rely on this as a sedation. It is advisable that on the day of healing, you refrain from placing foodstuff in your system for a minimum of an hour before the healing process. It is desirable also for all healers to consume as much vegetable juices and apple juice as they can, for these tend to vitalize the system in a natural manner. A simple diet adhered to will greatly affect your ability to transfer this great force through you to the recipient. Fruit is quite desirable as it is very useful in tuning the nervous system. Grain oil is the bread of life. You must realize that grain oil, if taken in proper quantities, will furnish you with the chemicals required for vibrant health. Pure grain oil will extend life expectancy by at least twenty to thirty percent and therefore, each of you should consume grain oil daily. Unsaturated fats are desirable. Moreover, a certain percentage of these must be consumed each day as they serve to cleanse the blood vessels. The troublesome fats and undigested sugars, being detrimental elements, are absorbed and cleansed from the system. Basically, if one adheres to these dietary precautions, one will find an energy returning to them such as they have not had since early youth.

Also, many of you on your plane do not realize how closely your thoughts and actions are tuned with ours and how much your prayers mean to us and how much your tears hold us back. Prayer is a supplication from the heart. We on this plane pray and pray and pray, even as you do on your plane. We can rise by your prayers as much as we can by the deeds that we do here. Prayer is so important. And your prayers are heard. They are not always answered because sometimes the answer would be wrong and not for your good. You are disappointed when this happens and say, 'Oh, my prayers are not answered.' This is not so. Your prayers are all heard. They are listened to and answered where it will do good. We hear you when you pray for healing and in this we try to help. We would ask that when you pray for healings, you ask for a doctor and we will send in the doctor who is best fitted for the particular entity. We have many doctors here who are anxious to help. They cannot help unless they are asked. If only people would realize this it would be better for all.

*   *   *

In the next paragraph, Spirit is talking to the group who sat in the darkness, in meditation to aide Reverend Robert E. Wagner as he received these transcripts for the benefit of our fellowman. I include it so that you may have some insight into how you can be rewarded for your good works.

*   *   *

Your healings are slow but they are through and they are healings. You are gifted with the touch. Your hands are healing hands. All in this room have healing hands. This does much good for humanity. If only more people knew of this group they could be helped. You do much good and in the future will continue to do much good. The more healings you perform the deeper your gift becomes and the more able you are to heal. We are interested in all that is done in this group. You have prevented much illness; illness which would have come had these people not received healings by this group. You have prevented much pain and suffering and for this you will be blessed. You will all come over on a high plane. You will not have to go through the basic or intermediate steps; you will all be on a high level when you come over to our side. Your records will be written in gold; they will shine with the white light. We cannot say this of many groups but this group, though it is small, is blessed

Chapter 6

Thought

THOUGHT IS THE bread of the light. It is the very thing that life is dependent upon. On this plane of existence, you consume low grade thoughts. Even plants and animals have a vibratory rate. You require a proper combination of these various thought elements to nourish your body so that you can, through the thought process, contact us.

This contact then, is merely a transfer of thought or life. Every thought that you have is a creation of life or a transfer of life from one to another, for without thought there is no life. Dwell on this for a moment and you will realize the validity of this statement, for it takes thought to activate matter. The thought is the activating element, therefore, thought is life; thought is fuel for life; thought is the bread of life.

Now you know of the bread; you know of the transfer of thought. You also must know of the water; of the waters that you drink. One requires both bread and water to live. Now water is what? Since thought is life and water nourishes, then water is the motivating force behind the thought. The whole key to power is the motivating force behind the thought. This gives the thought direction; this gives the thought purpose and without a purpose and without a direction, thought can go astray. Once you have a balance of motive and thought you flourish. You can grow as a flower. You are like a bud that has not unfolded and may lay dormant because you have placed restrictions on your motives.

When you have a motive or a combination of motives with proper direction, you find that you become exhilarated. You become less aware of self and more aware of the needs of those around and about you and as you become lost in the needs of what is going on around and about you, you find yourself forgetting self and suddenly the individual road blocks that you face find a way of caring for themselves and dissolving before your eyes.

This is important, for as you dwell on the so called problem, you dissipate energy in this direction and you give this thought nourishment. You increase it's magnitude; you increase it's power; you increase it's potential in creation. So you can magnify a minor incident by your own engrossment in this minute condition and create a mountain of energy or a great obstacle to progress. It is purely by your own creation that many of these minor incidents become of great magnitude, for you have set the conditions and created the force which caused these minor incidents to become great. And by the same token, you can take a minor blessing and directed properly, can create a great love force which will overcome any negative force that surrounds you.

So inadvertently, you create, or let us say, you foster the problems you face. It becomes imperative that when one is faced with a difficulty, one must analyze this condition at a lower level of thought and examine the purpose of this obstacle. You are never placed in a position without a purpose. We will always, because of our love for the individual and for the purpose which we wish to establish, place minor incidents in your path as a warning to examine your thought process and from these obstacles, we hope to guide you in the right direction. When you understand the purpose of these obstacles, you will understand that you must examine them and derive from these conditions the wisdom or the deviation in the direction we wish to portray.

You have within your grasp, the ability to create vast potential power; the same potential power that the Christ Force demonstrated with Jesus of Nazareth, for He learned how to intensify this thought process. He would take a minor thought and if it was necessary for the welfare of those around and about Him, He would magnify this minor thought a thousand fold and then a thousand fold again. This explains the miracle of the bread and fishes; this explains His command of the elements. Many people wonder at this power and wonder; if one ever existed who could invoke this power. Many wonder if this is but a myth. It is no myth.

This identical power is available to each and every one on your plane. Each and every one has spirit companions who are working with them. The life nourishment of these companions is dependent on the thoughts created by the individual for thoughts are food for them. They need you and you need them for you are interdependent. So do not feel that you are annoying them or abusing them when you request that they work in the direction which you indicate by your thoughts. The more use you make of these forces, the more nourishment you feed them the more they grow and the closer you become to their vibratory level. This allows you to grow together for they in turn examine you and correct minor flaws within your thought pattern and thus become ultimately as one with you. You gain confidence in spirit and yourself through the full knowledge that this great force is there constantly to use. As you strengthen a muscle, by proper usage and not abuse, you find this muscle will be well toned and strengthened. So when you have proper thoughts combined with proper desire, you have fed your loved ones in the spirit world their food and they grow stronger.

When someone says, 'I give you food for thought,' they inadvertently speak the basic spiritual truth, for thought is food and direction is the water; the water that sustains life. Knowing the capacity; knowing the potential and knowing the fostering of life should be sufficient to cause you to ponder on these things and glean the basis of your very existence. Know that you are all creators. Jesus of Nazareth said, "My Father and I are one." He said in essence; 'I am like my Father. He can create and visualize; He can foster. He can direct and under His direction I can do likewise.' With this vast potential in the grasp of your hands, controlled properly, there is no limitation to what you can create and foster.

Examine your thought process for your thought process controls your advancement and your advancement controls life. On many occasions you inadvertently, through ignorance, (and we call ignorance sin), create a negative force and you can foster this negative force just as easily as you can foster a positive force. One you call God like and the other you call the devil. Remember this. remember it well.

Chapter 7

Light

ONE MUST UNDERSTAND the nature of light. Light is vibration. You can live in light or you can live in darkness. You can change the vibration which causes light, which when reduced becomes sound. Reduced even more this vibration becomes heat and reduce it yet again and it becomes a solid. So your physical is actually light reduced to a lower vibratory plane.

Out of the darkness comes light. This statement was made at the beginning and the beginning was thought and this thought manifested itself and as it grew in intensity the vibration grew causing an even greater intensity. It is known by your scientific minds that the higher the vibration the more intense the light. When you see spirit entities you see them initially as lights, for their vibration has risen to this level. As these entities evolve to a higher vibration they evolve to a higher plane of existence and as their thought forms expand you see form for the more advanced these entities become the more definite their thought patterns portray themselves. Likewise with you; you may live on a material plane and may be living in darkness emotionally. As you are enlightened, you overcome the restrictions of darkness and your avenues of expression expand to greater latitudes and your influence among others does likewise. As you become enlightened, you overcome your fear and anxiety; you become more positive in your actions and you become more tolerant of the frailties of those around and about you.

You readily recognize the frailties of others but rather than react to them you understand their weaknesses and act accordingly. We wish to have you enlightened as to your reason for being here. Many of you have been on the earth plane prior to your present transition and have experienced various emotional upsets and have not made accomplishments to your satisfaction. Most of you are back here because you have compassion for your fellowman who has been back here. You wish to come back to enlighten him as to the importance of spiritual existence. You wish to raise the vibration of your fellowman as to the importance of spiritual existence. You wish to raise the vibration of your fellowman to a higher plane of thought so that he can overcome his alleged materialistic thinking. You wish to bring back the information which will be helpful to mankind. This can be verified once again by your scientific minds. It is a known factor that the average vibratory rate of man is now considerably higher than it was a hundred years ago, two hundred years ago or two thousand years ago. Generally, your vibratory rate, as a group, elevates closer to our plane of existence each succeeding generation. There are those close to our plane of existence who are sent to you to be your leaders. We carefully tune in to your vibratory rate so that we may ascertain your level of understanding and speak to you at that level. There are many with sufficient background and previous experience, interested in elevating themselves again to the plane from which they have departed and they wish to carry many with them to higher planes of thought.

Thought is light but on a very high frequency. It's frequency is beyond your range of sight. You call this ultrasonics. In ultrasonics, you produce a vibration beyond your audible ear's capacity to hear and your visual capacity to see but this is the wave length which we use to descend to the individual who is tuned into our plane. There are those among you who can raise their vibratory rate to a level high enough so that we can contact them. Pure thought is a vibration. The words in the interpretation are of your making. Pure thought from our realm of existence is audible from time to time as a fluctuating sound; the means of interpretation being caused by the needs of those to whom the thought wishes to be conveyed. The thought is identical to everyone regardless of where they are in the universe. However, the interpretation is in accordance with the individual. Light then is thought; light is heat; light is sound; light is vibration and light is love. That is why when the great love force penetrates your being, some call it the great cosmic force. It warms you physically or your physical has been raised in vibration above it's normal level.

And in the process, you accelerate the flow overcoming the chance of any negative flow and this causes your vibration to become harmonious This is the basis of healing. For if your vibration pattern is in harmony you have health. If there is a discord or interference in the vibration pattern within your aura this reflects in your physical. Likewise, the thought patterns which cause any disharmony or lack of enlightenment in you spiritual being can, through the overwhelming love force, be brought into harmony again and you can reverse the process of this disharmony. And depending upon your ability to retain this love force, you determine whether this harmonious vibration remains continuous or whether you revert to your former patterns of thinking. For you are thought; you are light and vibration and you are the reflection of your thought patterns.

You are lights. When we see you from where we are we see you as you see us; that is as lights. You have various colors and intensities but you are lights and are seen as such. When there is one amongst you that can intensify this light to a level which is brilliant by your standards, we are attracted to this light and work constantly to communicate through this source to give you the wisdom which we have accumulated.

Remember that you are thought; that you are not only a material being but that you are also spiritual and that you can transfer thoughts readily amongst yourselves as well as amongst others who are not in the physical condition. There is no difference in communicating between yourselves and communicating with us (spirit), the process is identical. This may surprise you but your ego is identical to ours whether you are in the physical or in spirit. This has not and will not change. You purify yourselves but you never change. You elevate yourself but you are a part of what you call the God-force. Each of you is an essential part of this great force and concentrate it in any direction that you see fit. It is available to any individual who has a firm desire to use this force FOR THE BENEFIT OF those around and about them.

Chapter 8

Building Your Future

THE REMAINS ARE being uncovered now which were built by a former civilization at the head of the Nile. They have been buried in the sand and preserved for thousands of years. You see, we made the same mistake back then that you are almost making now. We turned a fertile valley into a desert, for we were concerned primarily with what we could derive for our own personal gain giving no thought to the welfare of others, and consequently, we have not and received not.

Mankind today is aware of our foolishness. Mankind is aware not only of the folly of being self centered but he is learning to look for the realities of life. We have come back from time to time to convince our fellowman of the foolishness of self centeredness, for through our selfishness we rendered ourselves fertile one day and within the span of eight generations found ourselves void of sustenance. There is a great movement throughout your world to overcome this tendency in your thinking. Do not resist this movement otherwise you will be consumed by it. For it is through this movement that we are preparing the way for the 'second coming' of the 'second manifestation' of your Christ Spirit.

This coming has been predicted and it shall be. Within the next two decades you well see a general mounting of the crescendo of this movement (Keep in mind these dissertations were received between 1971 & 1973). Man's worship of material possession will devour those who worship thusly and those who worship the needs and wants of their fellowman will be strengthened; lifted and exalted. You will see the second coming, as you call it, within the matter of twenty years. (Meaning now!) The way is being prepared at this moment. Listen well, for the reality of life is your thought. The only reality is thought. YOU ARE WHAT YOU THINK. YOU CAN MANIFEST ANY IMAGE YOU CHOOSE. You can become anything you desire providing you think properly in this direction. You do not will yourself to be what you desire, rather you train yourself to think in the manner which will create the condition you desire. If you wish to think along lines which are proper to become a barrister you will become one. However, if you merely state, 'I wish to be a barrister' and do not cause your thinking to change along these lined, you will never become one.

You become that which you desire providing you put forth the effort and providing you open your heart and your mind to receive the instructions which those on the other side who are interested in your progression will provide. They insert the proper thoughts to you and you build upon these thoughts the same as you build a building. One thought at a time you build a firm foundation and then add proper thoughts again one at a time and the results is the same as you build a building; that is by laying one brick at a time.

Ultimately, you have a beautiful structure. You can lay bricks and build a jail or you can lay bricks and build a cathedral or you can lay bricks and build an office, home or factory. This is your choice. You attract to you the ones from the other side who are interested in furthering themselves through working with you. For by helping you they advance. They can only receive by giving and this is a lesson that you must learn well. You must not wait until you get to this plane of existence to learn this simple lesson. You receive by giving. You are as you think not as you envision yourself.

Remember that you are a light and that we identify your desire by the colors you emit for since each phase of thought has it's own corresponding color we know your thinking by looking at your aura. Your aura changes from day to day and from hour to hour depending on your thinking as of any given moment. So if you have a legal problem and send up a thought desirous of legal advice, those over here who are versed in the legal profession will recognize this light and will come to you and will either speak to you or through you depending on the circumstances. And an hour later, needing medical advice, if you but change your thought process to this new avenue, your aura will change or the color of your light will change and a doctor or lawyer will be attracted to you and once again will respond to this avenue of expression.

Use these people; feed these people for they live on thought and love and service. This is their food the same as the food that you eat or consume to support your physical body.

You can be contented with being lost in this existence and not make any particular progress or you can intensify your light through service to others and shine brighter than those around and about you and suddenly the restrictions which have been holding you back will fall off of your shoulders, hands and arms and you will become free of encumbrances and you will know no fear, for fear is evil. Everything that is evil is a derivative of fear. Love is harmony. Dwell in love and advance yourself in love. Love will free you of all shackles. Love is concern not for yourself but for the needs of those around and about you; not concern for there desires but for their needs. The rewards are great for those who serve us (spirit) for we will open doors which you could not open of your own volition.

It is important that you know yourself. It is important that you be honest with yourself for you are what you have made yourself at this moment and will be what you make of yourself tomorrow and the tomorrow after tomorrow. You have complete control of your destiny. There is nothing impossible to the one who will open his heart to this great love force.

Chapter 9

Jacob's Ladder

MANY OF YOU will remember the story of Jacob's Ladder. This was a vision which indicated that you attain your contact with the God-head one step at a time. Thus if a lesser entity makes contact to assist you he is nevertheless part of the God-head and is on the ladder of communication as determined by his own individual attainment.

Many of you are on different rungs of the ladder and many of you will have already stepped up many rungs of the ladder. It has been said that there are seven planes of existence but this is not true. There are seven times seven times seven and you can multiply this to infinity because there are that many planes. There may be basic divisions but everyone ascends to a higher plane ultimately. In this connection, there is another fallacy which should be dispelled. Once you have attained a certain level of existence you cease to have a desire to help other entities and suddenly find yourself desirous of personal self attainment. Now this is contrary to the law for in order to advance, you must lose your self awareness and with compassion and the desire to serve those around and about you, you overcome this. You must overcome selfish motivations for this is sin.

Many masters have stated that you were born in sin but you are born, basically, in ignorance of the law. When you first come back or return to the earth plane, you have a basic, pure concept of life. Later you find yourself in an environment of entities who are overcome by self motivated thoughts. Here we are talking of reincarnation. So when we speak of being born in sin we speak of being born in self-esteem; self-centered motivations. Some call this the devil. The devil is merely a misuse of the love force. The force itself is all powerful but you direct this force whether it be for good or evil. The force is greater now than it was at the time of the former Masters. That is why Jesus of Nazareth spoke in this manner, 'greater things than I, you can do also,' and this is so.

It is not unusual for us to plan four or five generations ahead to create an atmosphere which will be conducive to proper contact. It isn't by accident that all the great minds recently available for space exploration were placed on your planet. Remember this well, for we planned it. It is not by accident that your so called hippy movement was worldwide. This movement transcends all ideologies and I use the word properly. It will unify the world, as you call it. within the next one and one half decades. This movement will transcend all national pride as it was predicted on many occasions by the prophets.

You may call these forces at will. Many different people will have different terminologies, but the force is the same. Whether one asks for the great violet ray to come in and consume or whether one asks for the great healing force to come in to heal it is immaterial because it is the same force. The important condition in this situation is not what you name this great force but rather what your motivation is. For the strength of your motivating thought determines the strength of the force which flows through you or is directed by you. It is not necessary that this force flow through the individual entity. It can be directed by the entity to another person but this is far more difficult. When you have attained a level of advancement sufficiently high; when you have climbed up many more steps of that golden ladder, you will be in a position to direct the force rather than have it flow through you. However, since this force flowing through you harmonizes your own condition, it is desirable that you request this force to flow through you as you are assisting others. There is no one who is inherently gifted. There are those sent down to your plane of existence who are far advanced this is true but anyone can attain this same level with the same effort.

When we wish something accomplished, we look among the entities available and assign those chosen to go down the ladder to your plane of existence to demonstrate to you and show you and talk to you in a manner in which we wish them to. They do not lose their identity, that is, they are still individuals. You never lose your individuality when you ascend to the God-force. You never become a sword as some intimate. You become more refined and as you ascend you become more capable of lateral movements of influence. Those who are chosen to assist those less fortunate are not unhappy because they are sent down; they anticipate the assistance which they can convey to you helping you to advance to a higher level.

This is a continuous process. The vibratory rate of your human temples has increased three fold since the day of Moses; two fold since the day of Jesus of Nazareth and one fold since the day of Mahatma Gandhi. This is the reason why the average entity today has more tools to work with to accomplish the desired ends, for man had elevated his general intelligence to a higher plane of existence. In other words, the general elevation of the common group on your planet is many rungs up the ladder; Jacob's Ladder.

Chapter 10

Purpose

WE HAVE OUTLINED previously that life is thought; that thought is vibration and that thought has no dimension which is fixed. Thought can be dispersed or it can be concentrated. Thought is the only reality of life. All light is the result of thought. This is how we can contact you. We send out a thought pattern and contact your entity and using your thought we exercise the known centers and cause you to hear, see and feel various aspects of our being. This is merely a means of transferring ideas or thoughts. We create a vision, that is, we use vibration to build up mutations. First you must be familiar with that which we build up so that you will recognize the objects which we contribute for your use. Thought is pure; thought knows no bounds. Thought has no limitations and thought can be either dispersed and become weak or thought can be concentrated and become the strongest force available.

The control of the intensity and the direction of thought is the choice of the entity. When seen together we see you as a cluster of lights. You look not unlike what you call your aurora borealis, for this is what is familiar to all of you. These thought patterns, as given out by you, cause various colors such as the rainbow, to flash out from your star in a pattern. As your thoughts change, the coloring pattern changes as it emanates from you and consequently, we know your every thought. This is why the Master Teacher spoke of your Father knowing your needs and your wishes before you utter them. This is our device for recognizing thoughts. We do know your needs, for in examining your spectrum, we see the patterns of your thoughts. To those who are bright enough (meaning your light is bright enough) to gain our attention, we will endeavor to send forces to further strengthen their patterns and as each force attaches to the individual aura, both gain in power. Ultimately, this individual becomes merely a focal point around which many auras or entities of auras cluster. Eventually, you evolve a new entity which is all inclusive and all powerful. This is basic; there is not an individual who is not capable of ascending to the proper heights individually. We have individuals on this plane of existence and they strengthen themselves by their attractions.

In order to strengthen yourself then, you must have a purpose. In order to find the inner peace and in order to find the augmenting forces which will assist you to overcome the limitations which you have erroneously placed upon yourself by your evil influences, you must lose yourself in the needs of those around and about you or lose yourself in a purpose or a direction which you wish to concentrate upon. In either case, you are serving and directing the needs of those around and about you. There is no one individual who is sufficient unto himself.

This is why all the masters recognized the great universal force. The universal force is an accumulation of forces with a common purpose. If your desire, will or purpose is strong enough and the issue is pure enough, you can contact sufficient small groups of small forces which in turn will form a nuclei for greater groups of forces and ultimately, you will have a great force available at any given moment.

So it is quite important that the need or purpose be proper to attract the forces that perform the so called miraculous acts. Do not make the mistake of attempting to use this great accumulation of force to better your individual ego or lust for we do not recognize sin as reality. Ego, fear, lust and awareness of self are all evil forces or sin; all of these generally, are disharmony. All of these are generally caused by losing your contact with your spiritual self. You lose contact with your spiritual self when your vibration level has regressed to a level sufficiently low in vibration to cause your material thinking to be of prime importance. When you concentrate on satisfying your ego and lust, this is evil or sin.

When people say you were born in sin you can understand the statement now. You are born in awareness of the flesh conditions around you. You are aware of the sense of security in another at birth. You rely strongly on the material needs of your physical and on the security of someone caring for you physically. The sensations of touch and sound become real as you begin to ignore the reality of the thought that causes all of these sensations. It is like a disease. You treat the symptoms of disease. To you, the symptoms of erroneous thinking are reality while you ignore the cause of the erroneous thinking that is the disharmony in your vibration pattern.

A harmonious spiritual existence is essential to your ascension. Once you become fully aware that you are merely a composite of electrons which are vibrating at a low rate of speed and that these electrons constitute your flesh life, then these electrons are under the full surveillance and control of your spirit entity. If you fear it reflects; if you love it reflects and if you hate it reflects.

You must understand that for every force there is a compensating force and an opposing force. There is, as you would call it, a series of checks and balances. For those who are familiar with music, you know from experience that certain cords, certain groups of notes which form cords, have a mutual sound that is harmonious and that if you disturb this relationship you have a disharmony which is quite shattering to some individuals.

That is why certain entities are attracted to certain other entities. It is because they are in harmony. They are not necessarily the same tone value but they are in harmony with this other vibration and this is why certain groups form to create common goals and accomplishments. It is not wrong for certain individuals to be in disharmony with other individuals, but in order for this individual to be effective he should seek out those who will harmonize with him and they too will find themselves in a harmonious relationship. What I am saying is, if one does not harmonize with you it does not necessarily make them wrong or you right. If they do not harmonize with you it is evident that you do not harmonize with them.

A rose in the middle of a field of dandelions is a weed, but a dandelion field as such is beautiful. There are no weeds; there are misplaced people. That is why it is well that when you do not harmonize with someone you seek out those whom you harmonize with, for there are many, many chords and groups of chords in a symphony.

Vibration is thought. Thought creates vibration. Vibration is the means of transferring energy from one plane to another. You are generators of thought. You have a power available to you as individuals. You can harness this great concentration of thought or you can fail to tap this inner power and live a futile existence. The choice is yours. When you overcome sin you are reborn in spirit and remove the shackles of sin, for in spirit there is no limitation to the availability of thought power, It is only your materialistic, sensual thinking which limits your capacity to use and direct the great powers which are available to you. Only you, as an individual, are capable of triggering this great force. You as an individual act as a triggering device and can create a force as powerful as any nuclear explosion. If you were to study the principles of nuclear physics, you would understand the forces available to you through spiritual power. Your spiritual involvement operates on the same principle as nuclear fusion. Understand that thought, motivation and knowing both that you are merely a part of a great force and that you can control, tap and use this great force at will (providing your purpose and direction is strong in that direction) are fundamental.

Chapter 11

The Promise

I AM ABOUT to make a statement which some of you will accept and some of you, because of your training, will find rather difficult to comprehend. The day of the crucifixion was the anniversary of the man called Jesus. He was crucified on His birthday and this is as it was predicted by the prophets. As planned by the priests, the crucifixion took place on the Sabbath, for they knew that this was the day when people would be in the streets and that this was also the day when this devout man would, according to tradition, attend the synagogue of His choosing. They knew that He would come to them. Many of these people knew that they had no choice in the matter. They were overwhelmed by a force which was greater than their force. This was willed from above.

By your standards of time, the anniversary of the death and the birth were both approximately the 12th day of the month of April in which you now count your time. He was born and crucified at dusk. If this had not happened, you would not know yourselves as you do at the moment. You would be living in basic sin. Jesus was sent here to show you the way. He was sent here to demonstrate the law which the prophets before Him told you about. But you ignored their prophesies. They demonstrated immortality; they demonstrated that there are no chosen ones and they preached ceaselessly that each individual has the same capacity to communicate with and tap into the great spirit forces which are available to each and every one for their use.

He did not say that the power of God was in Him, but rather that the power of God worked through Him. Read companion books and you will find similar utterances of others. He demonstrated in such a way that, through His actions you were convinced of the validity of His statements.

THIS IS THE PROMISE. IF YOU HAVE IMPLICIT FAITH IN YOUR LIGHT, WHICH IS GOD, AND YOU HAVE COMPLETE FAITH THAT YOU CAN TAKE THIS SPARK OF LIGHT AND AUGMENT IT A THOUSAND TIMES AND AS YOU AUGMENT THIS LIGHT YOU ATTRACT TO THIS LIGHT THE GREAT FORCES AVAILABLE TO THOSE AROUND AND ABOUT YOU, FURTHER AUGMENTING THIS FORCE, ULTIMATELY, YOU CAN BE CONTROLLING A FORCE GREATER THAN THE ELEMENTS.

You as individuals are gods. You are part of the Great I Am and when you meditate you must meditate knowing full well that you are, according to your light, capable of ascending to a point at which this great love force can contact you and give you peace and wisdom. There is but one path and you must not waver in your thoughts for there are no deviations from this path. You must send your wishes or prayers to the Great Head, the Great I Am and at His choosing, in the light of His vast wisdom, He will assign the proper forces to you and these forces will be sufficient to handle the situation whether you are seeking aid for self or another. In each instance, you receive in proportion to your giving until you arrive at that level where your will to give overwhelms those limitations which you have placed upon yourself. This force then multiplies many, many fold.

So it was in the beginning and will be until life without end. You ask yourself, 'is there a second coming of the Master Teacher?' This question seems to be quite prevalent. It seems as though the people on your plane of existence are in a turmoil. They are actually willing a catastrophe upon themselves in the hope that they will help bring this about. They may not ultimately say so but there is an underlying force which we recognize here as being such and this is true. Man has lived in sin long enough. It is time that he overcomes sin and ascends to the level of existence which is above pettiness, jealousy, ego, lust and self esteem for these are all sin. What you imagine to be sin or crime is the result of these basic emotions. All of your crime stems from one or a combination of these emotions. There are many variations of these stages of self esteem, self satisfaction and lust. Awareness of flesh which reaches the stage of worship is sin.

Many of the prophets spoke of the immortality of the soul but none demonstrated this great immortality until the Master Teacher demonstrated it. There will be another prophet called who will again give you further enlightenment into the Great Love Force. His words will enrage and he will be considered mad at first but eventually people will listen. They will listen more carefully and will comprehend that this one IS NOT the chosen one. However, contrary to what you read in the Book (Bible), Jesus of Nazareth was not the chosen one. You attain these levels through diligence.

It is true, not to offend the teaching which you have received, that there were those who chose to descend to your level of existence in the anticipation that they could develop at your vibration to a level sufficiently high to enable them to become a vehicle through which this great force could speak. Jesus of Nazareth was only one of these who descended from the heavens, as you call it, and entered the flesh. Others descended also with the same purpose in mind but unfortunately, when they became acclimated to this plane of existence they discovered that they had not overcome the sin level, the consciousness of flesh, and consequently did not elevate to a proper vibration. There are some who come down to this plane from the higher realm who almost accomplish their expressed self but few accomplish this plateau. I wish to remind you that everyone is part of God; everyone has the capacity within themselves to augment the power. Everyone who has this God power is capable of infinite intelligence, action and activity. All the Master Teacher wished to do was to dispel the reality of the realism of material vibration. Material vibration is the lowest level of spirituality and is only in your mind's eye.

Now, we see you as lights varying in color and intensity. As you build your vibratory rate the intensity of your illumination augments itself and attracts forces in proportion to your vibrations. Remember this well, for as you build your vibration you build up the effectiveness of your contact with the higher forces.

In order to activate these forces, you must have a motive, faith and purpose and be so overwhelmed by the need of the one before you that you lose consciousness of self. Once you have accomplished this, then you will have succeeded in knowing that you are a part of God. When you pray, pray to God, pray to the source of all light, pray to that which is all and is all in all and expect a response. Quiet yourself, lose yourself, anticipate the beauty of ascension and do not waiver. You will never be harmed by those in the levels which we represent. You will only benefit with the ascension to the light and when you ascend to this great light, you will have a complete, harmonious condition around and about you.

Chapter 12

Vibration

THE POWERS WHICH are available to all at all times can be used or abused; used for good or evil. Therefore, you must have the proper motivating approach. Once your motive is established; once you humble yourself to the point where you can see that the great force is using you merely as a vehicle through which it flows; once you have removed all fear and doubt and concern from your countenance you have become a vehicle through which the great force will flow freely to serve the needs of those around and about you.

But the gift is ours to remove also, for you make yourself worthy of our indulgence and if you cease to make yourself worthy we find those who are worthy and we by-pass the unworthy. And if you have been bathed in the light and have made perfect contact with your higher self in the higher planes and this contact is denied you;—THIS IS A FATE AS HORRIBLE AS ONE CAN EXPERIENCE. This happens when you abuse this gift that has been given you. You must take care of it.

Now, this great force is a vibration. This great force has many harmonics which vary with the needs of the individual for it manifests itself in a myriad of patterns. It is the force that causes the growth of every animate and inanimate object on your earth plane and throughout your known universe. Actually, there are no inanimate objects in your environment. Every object manifested is a living expression of what you call the God Force. Because it is vibrating at a certain rate; it has certain harmonics. It takes form and as long as this vibration pattern remains as such, the visual conditions of the object will remain as you see them. Now you know, for many of you have studied the so called sciences, that when heat is added or taken from a so called inanimate object it changes form. When you breathe in water (moisture), you lower the vibration and when you breath out it becomes vapor. You lower it still further and it becomes steam. I can repeat this with stone. Stone breathes the same as you breathe. It's devices are different but it breathes.

You manufacture what you call cement which is stone that has had it's moisture removed from it at a high temperature. You place this dehydrated stone in the presence of water again and you get a very powerful reaction; it creates sensible heat and returns to stone as you know it. You see, every natural condition when allowed to be in it's normal harmonic condition, will revert to it's normal shape or form.

This explains the principles of health. Your mind has an image that you have acquired through many incarnations and as you develop, you remove certain discords at will from your harmonic condition and this reflects materially in your temple. You have the complete power within your mental frame to change your appearance. You have certain external influences but these you can control. Many people associate themselves with people who do not harmonize with them. These people may be in perfect harmony within themselves but they cause a discord when they are in your proximity. This reflects in like manner in your being and consequently, those who associate with you do affect your general thought pattern arrangement and your physical appearance which is merely a mirror of your thought patterns.

So, if you wish to be a beautiful woman or a handsome man, inside as well as outside, it behooves you to associate with beautiful people and gradually you will acquire their aura. You have the will to change your experiences in life depending on your approach or your mental attitude. You will not come into contact with us directly until you have acquired the proper attitude. When you have opened yourself to us and we are aware of the sincerity of your condition, we will work through you freely and great works will be caused to happen because you have created a pure vehicle for us to use.

We do the work and you focus our attention. You are the spearhead; you are the light; you are the flashlight; if you wish to visualize yourself as such, and you mentally attract us and cause us to see in a direction of need and then we perform.

Now the Great I Am is all, in all and through all. You can assist those around and about you by maintaining a mental image of perfection and if this image of perfection is directed to this entity, it will with your unwavering direction projected, cause it to indulge this entity. We will ferret out the discordant areas in the vibratory patterns and replace them with the proper harmonics but you must maintain this image for quite some time, for it takes time for your material being to replenish itself. Your material being; your temple produces between three and four thousand new cells every day. You must have the proper elements in your system so that these new cells can be replenished in a proper chemical content. People age not so much by their bodies deteriorating but primarily because of their change in attitude and change in eating habits and vitality within the system.

When one is young, one has simple trust and enthusiasm, but as one matures one becomes resigned to the fact that, 'this is all there is to life so we might just as well coast with it taking out of it what we can take getting as little exercise as we can get away with because that is effort, and therefore, one ages rapidly. But if you have an attitude that is useful, you then have yourself the proper chemicals and receive the proper amount of exercise so that the toxins in your system can be disposed of as they were in your youth. Therefore, you would never age physically. I cannot emphasize this firmly enough—THE AGING PROCESS IS A CHANGE OF MENTAL IMAGING. You become lazy; you become careless of your food intake; you want the luxuries and these luxuries are what cause you to age. So, if you want to maintain a youthful appearance or if you wish to regain a youthful appearance, you must have enthusiasm; you must anticipate today and tomorrow; you must look to the needs of those around and about you and lose yourself in their needs—lose yourself—your self awareness is a nail in your coffin. Self indulgence and self awareness are the two greatest sins.

Sin is not a crime, as you call it; sin is ignorance of God's Law. Sin is ego; sin is indulgence; sin is lust. Sin and crime contribute to one another. One murders because of lust or ego. One steals because of lust or ego. You will find that behind all crime there is a self indulgent cause. Therefore, sin is the cause of crime. You will not be sinful if you lose yourself and in so doing, you give of you great love force. Love manifests in many ways. Love and affection are not synonymous. Very often affection is a part of lust; a means of satisfying one's ego. True love looses itself in those around and about you. By helping those around and about your love allows this emotion of service to be dominate. For when one gives freely of love one looses the aging wrinkles and one looses tendencies to all disease. I will make another statement—all disease organic or inorganic, is caused by improper imagery or improper emotion of the part of the individual. There are no exceptions.

When you play beautiful music and someone hits a note that does not harmonize with the other notes, you are aware of this and react to this. This, in essence is what happens to the individual health wise when they allow a discordant note; a discordant thought or trend of thought to enter their pattern. Think of yourself as a symphony that you are constantly working on for this is precisely what you are. You must remember that every member of your body, miraculously, if you wish to look at it properly, when it is injured, if you will allow it to heal itself normally it will take on precisely the same shape as that which it had before it was injured or before the injury took place.

Something somewhere somehow causes this to happen. It is this symphony that you have been composing, by your actions through your many incarnations, that caused your body to take a certain shape. For example, it is not unusual for someone to have stubby fingers and someone else to have long fingers. Most people say that is the way they were born and that is true. Now, you come into this plane of existence bringing with you this harmony at birth. You bring in with you this symphony, if you prefer to call it that and as you grow up, you add to and take away from this symphony.

I believe we have been searching for many, many moons for a means of describing the true entity which you are. We are trying to establish an attitude and understanding of the reality of life or origin of life, as you know it, and to further explain sudden death due to accident. You may be aware that if you took a symphony and suddenly jumbled all these beautiful chords, you would have a very discordant condition to the point where it could not re-arrange itself again and this is what you call death. I am not speaking of normal transition. That is why it takes some people who have been killed, as you call it, in armed conflict or in vehicle accidents or accidents of other natures, so long to re-harmonize this jumble to come back to speak and contact you again.

Man is suspicious of the so called unknown; man is suspicious of being assisted, for then he feels an obligation and this is unfortunate. But this will be overcome. Love for love's sake—you must give freely of love and be forgiving of the ignorance of those around and about you and be patient. Have much patience, for ultimately love will overcome. Yes, give love for love's sake. Others will ultimately overcome the same suspicions and will reflect this love.

Chapter 13

Principles of Life Form

THERE IS LIFE form throughout the universe. It manifests itself in a manner that is required by the environment that this life force finds itself involved. Life is thought, Life is energy concentrated in thought. Life is the electric spark which causes your physical or any condition you touch, to become motivated. You can transfer yourself to any object around and about you and transfer life to this object. You can, with thought, speak not in a manner which you understand, but you can, by thought transference, speak with every animate and inanimate object. I wish to correct the differentiation here; there is no inanimate object. Every object that you are exposed to has life. Whether it be metal, wood, stone or flesh; it is a form of life. They all vibrate at a level which caused them to take the physical appearance of what you see. You can take metal, freeze it; melt it and cause it to be a gas. For when you see metal transfer it's energy into a gas, it merely expands further; it vibrates at a higher rate and expands until you see it no more but it is there. When these same molecules, as you call them, slow down their vibration again, they become a molten state and then they become solid. You see, metal is animate; all is animate.

You as individuals, vibrate at a certain rate when you are flesh. If you increase your vibration, you can dissipate this flesh; you can cause this flesh to become vapor through your thought processes. You could transfer these vapors through walls and place yourself in a different environment and mentally slow your vibration down to it's former level and cause it to become visible again to the material eye. Now, this is the truth of life. Every object and any object can do likewise. This may amaze you but it is basic. Every object is motivated by what you call electric force. The unseen! This force can be separated from your material and when you speak of the spark of life departing from the flesh by accident, it merely means that the motivating force which activated your flesh has departed from the flesh and allowed the flesh to become inert matter.

The internal force which you call the spark of life is that which you see as a light when you see an entity. It is the triggering force which controls your physical. Now there is an external force which causes the metal to heat up to increase it's vibratory rate until it becomes molten, vapor, gas and or be invisible. Take the external stimulating force away from this molten metal and it will regress to solid. Every object has a history of this nature. You take stone as we stated before; you mine stone; you pulverize stone; you dehydrate this stone; you put it in sacks and store this stone and when you take this stone and place it in a bin and mix it with water it generates great heat and it goes back again to it's natural state as stone. But, here again is an external force which causes this to become fact. I give you these examples for this is essential to life.

You are sparks; you are lights—I spoke of this before. When we observe your light, your light takes on various colors; various combinations of colors an various intensities depending on your motivated desire at that moment. You have the power within you to cause this light to increase in intensity until it glows as brilliant as a star. We recognize this light and we see the colors and those who are attracted to that phase of life. Life has as many phases as you have hair on your head. This light attracts spirit entities and they come to this light source as a moth is attracted to a flame but these are not consumed by the flame. These entities come and augment this force and as each one joins in this force they increase this intensity further. They increase the vibratory rate higher and they attract more and more and more until you discover that like atomic energy, a small spark will suddenly become a great force. This spark has attracted to it, at times, millions of forces; millions of entities, all with a common desire of service and this great force can and will perform the feat that is necessary to be performed at the moment. This may explain to you why the individual can generate this great power, for it is the combined power of many that flows through this focal point.

Each individual will understand in the light of their own experience and when the individual looses the awareness of self and does not fear loosing their identity and has a desire to become part of a great moving vital force then all will be as we wish it and you will find that you are not losing your identity but you are gaining and enlarging your sphere of influence. THIS IS THE ONLY WAY TO ASCEND You must overcome self esteem; you must humble yourself. Know that you are a part of a great spirit entity and be grateful that you are part of this entity and ask what you can do to be an efficient part so that this great motivating force can gain in stature and increase and increase in it's thoughts until it's mission is fulfilled.

The Christ Spirit is the over-all spirit form or the God form, as you wish to call it, for your particular planet. There are similar forms of spirit on every planet throughout the universe. This is an important factor to remember. Each individual in the world is part of this Christ form.

Lust and self esteem will cause individuals to bring their vibrations so low that they are not an efficient part of this great light form complex. They become as a scar tissue on a leaf. However, when the same individuals overcome their lust and self esteem, they ultimately will have overcome their material limitations and will, at will, elevate their higher self to this Christ Spirit level and do that which they are here for.

There are many facets and many needs in this great mass of spirit. It takes the cooperation of all to make this great spirit wholesome and effective. There are many who wish to ascend to this level of consciousness but they fear they must give up their so called material conveniences. Now this is a fallacy. Your temples or bodies are a means of expression. We do not desire that you deny yourself the normal emotional outlets in your life. Otherwise we would not give you flesh temples in the first place. You have dominion over that which is around and about you. It is your duty to care for that which is around and about you and it is your duty to perform the acts which you were placed here for as part of the great over-all entity and if you as an individual, do not perform these acts, you will find that you will encounter resistance from those around and about you and within yourself you will have frustrations and cause disharmony within your vibration pattern and this will be reflected in your aura.

Every thought form has it's own color value. That is why when we see your entity we see you as a multi colored light. We see you as a spectrum; an ever pulsating spectrum. As you advance to a higher plane you will receive purer thoughts and when you see visions you see clearer visions. At first you will hear voices and see symbols and things of this nature. As you progress, you will actually find yourself in great areas of beautiful influence, then you will receive pure thought and then ecstasy. Each has the ability, if they would but apply it, to ascend to this higher plane of existence for instruction and renewal of energy. This is your reason for meditating. We wish to emphasize the point that when you meditate it would be well for you to have a strong desire to ascend to the higher plane so that you may throw off the negative influence which you have partaken of from those around and about you. You can do this daily until you get to the level where these negative thoughts of those around and about you cannot penetrate. For you are emanating at a rate so great that they cannot break through to your forces. As you build up to your higher self, you make yourself more immune to negative forces and under these conditions, physical symptoms of erroneous thought patterns will disappear.

This will explain to you that when you have a strong desire to make yourself available for this great force to flow and to heal, it is merely the force of driving out the disharmony from the countenance of the one which is before you. You overwhelm this one with your great force and you bathe this one in this great force that is emanating through you. When you give a healing, do not cause yourself to be a passive vehicle through which the force can flow, but make yourself a powerful light and have a strong desire to raise to a higher plane so that you can tap a power greater than yourself. As atomic energy, you can augment this power; you can be the spark which causes a great force to expand and expand and flow through you and overwhelm the one who is to receive through you and to have the disharmonious vibrations erased from their countenance.

Breathing is essential and it is the depth and extremes of your breathing which causes it to be effective. Breathing will raise your vibration initially ten fold if it is done briefly. This is essential to perfect health.

Chapter 14

Let Your Light Shine

THE CHRIST SPIRIT is the spirit force of your world. Each individual is an essential part of this spirit force and is capable of raising his mentality to a level which will contact this Christ Spirit or force and do works likewise. This Christ Force also contacts greater forces. That is why the Father chose to work through this force. This force or Christ Spirit was humble and knew from whence it's power came. (Spirit is talking about Reverend Robert E. Wagner in this instance) All glory goes to God. We are only the vehicle used to carry out He's wishes.

If one could purify their thinking and remove all doubt, misgivings and selfish personal gain from their countenance they too could generate a thought and this thought would be the nucleus for a concerted action for it is the purity of your thought which determines the intensity of your light. As I said before, you are unlike stars to us. We see you as lights. I know I am repeating myself, but I wish to reemphasize the personal responsibility for the intensity of your light. If you wish to do great works you must purify your purpose and have a desire that surpasses the awareness of self. Then you will have tapped this great force and this great force will flow through you in ever increasing intensity.

You are thought and thought is the only real condition of life. Thought may manifest itself as the necessities of convenience demand. Your thought existence on this planet is as you see yourself and if you were on another planet you would assume the countenance and the purpose of life expression on these other planets. Each planet has it's own form of life expression. Each planet contributed to the over all life cycling of your universe and there are many millions of universes. So you have an infinite power of thought source available to you at all times.

We are only attracted to those whose light intensity is greater than that of the general masses of life. You are not unlike the milky way and that is why so many of you do not contact the higher elements readily because you are lost in what some people call the stream of life. You are content to let life pass you by and not have a purpose so you get lost in what we would call the milky way. We have other expressions but you are not at a level where you would understand our terminology so we must explain it to you in this manner. Everyone and every living element throughout the universe is interdependent.

Many of you have considered the reason for the colors around the planet Saturn. You know that this must be something other than just reflection of the light from the solar source and in this you are correct for Saturn, generally, is the storehouse of all the spirit entities when they first go across to the other side, as you call it. This is where they find themselves again and this is why you see the spectrum, for every vibration has a corresponding color in the spectrum. When one passes to the other realm, they go into this great pool and they rest and they come closer to the God power and then absorb, the same as you absorb on this plane, the needed spiritual elements or the needed thought structure to perfect themselves or cause themselves to rise to a higher plane of thought. When they have found themselves, they again wish to serve the Master and then choose the area in which they wish to express this new thought pattern for the benefit of those around and about them.

Now, only a small percentage will return with this purpose in mind and have the courage and the stamina to maintain contact and not be swallowed up once again in the doubts and sins of material thinking. They have been blessed; they have been released from fear and anxiety and they come back to show us the way.

If you would but understand that you have a force available to you as powerful as any atomic bomb ever conceived by man you would not fear the wiles of material minds. You must understand that you are thought; you are the accumulation of thought. Because of your thought patterns, you emit certain light continuities to us. Those of us on this side who wish to serve will flock to this light source and in the process of giving of ourselves, we elevate ourselves to a higher plane of existence. Every one has a selfish motive for being where they are, but the purpose of this motive is of the utmost importance. It is not wrong to have a selfish desire to rise to a higher plane of existence.

Let's call this a motivating force. You must have an intense desire to rise to your higher self. However, we have found that in order to realize this desire you must loose yourself completely in the desire to attain a higher plane of existence. You must give of yourself freely for it is only through giving of yourself that you will receive your rewards of the higher life. It is essential that you assist those around and about you for in cleansing their thoughts and purifying their hearts, you are purifying your thoughts and heart and in time you will find that you have built up a harmony around you and will have ascended to a higher plane of thought.

There is no relationship between physical embodiment and spiritual attainment. There is need for many phases of thinking to harmonize relationships on your planet. Therefore, it is essential that you have many planes of existence represented in the same group for progression; each of which is as essential as the other.

You have available to you this great love force which transcends all forces. You control that electricity which you have at your switch. You must flip the switch to tap this great source of power and then again the flow of this power is controlled by the capacity of the wire through which this current can flow. This is unlike you as individuals. You must increase your capacity to allow this great force to flow before it can flow freely. Like muscles on your physical, you can also increase the strength of your spirituality by exercising this great thought and this thought power can and will increase it's capacity subsequent to each action of good which has been performed by the individual. For after each good act there is a certain amount of harmonizing within the thought patterns of the individual. Ultimately, you become a pure vehicle through which the great thoughts can be transferred to those around and about you.

This is not an exclusive power in any individual on your plane, for each of you seeks this great elated feeling, as you would call it; each of you seeks the ability to tap this great vast knowledge; this pool of knowledge which we hold at a distance sufficient to make it an earnest effort for you to tap, for without a challenge you will not make the effort to attain this level of achievement. We purposely raise this level slightly each day and we draw mankind, in general, upward in this manner. We have accelerated mankind's advancement these last two decades and find that we can accelerate it even more in the next decade. Your so called animalistic instincts will not be in a majority of the thoughts but in the minority. This is as it was predicted in the 'good book'. Those who choose to harmonize will become more harmonious; will become more vivid in their capacity to enlighten those around them. Those who have done this will grow and those who have not will disintegrate. This is the death as spoken of in the Bible. We are not speaking of material life and material death. There is merely a change of condition. At your plane of existence there is no loss of matter, just a change of condition in matter. Therefore, there cannot be any death materially. There can only be death spiritually. Understand this, that those who think in terms of fear and hate and mistrust, stand the danger of internal destruction and a complete disintegration, while those who humble themselves and loose themselves in the needs of their loved ones (remember everyone is a loved one), will grow and grow and will be blessed in the spirit light.

When you have been bathed in spirit light, you will have been blessed with the Christ Spirit; the same Christ Spirit that blessed Jesus of Nazareth. This is the only baptism that we recognize here. When you have attained a level of desire of purpose to be bathed by this Christ Spirit, you are baptized by God and from that day on, your attitudes; your approaches will be as those of the disciples and your blessings will be great.

Chapter 15

Building a Healthy Temple

WHEN YOU ARE born you are a perfect spirit being and unfamiliar with the ways of the material world. You have your idealistic approaches; you are born into a physical being which has not developed materially sufficient to respond to your whims and your desires as you would have it at first. You must take this physical being and train it to do your will and to function as you would have it function for this physical being is your responsibility. You chose it. In fact, you chose the parents, the physical parents through which this fetus was born or caused to be fertilized, if you wish to use the word, and you were the one who chose the instant and the conditions under which you adhered yourself to this physical mechanism. You, as a spirit entity who wishes to return to this phase of life to assist your progression or primarily to assist those around and about you, hover around flesh entities and you choose the ones through whom you wish to express yourself. At the moment of your choosing, you enter into the sperm which fertilized the egg and then you from that moment on, control the activities of this fertilized egg.

Now, there are times, and you must understand this well, that there are two spirit entities who almost simultaneously choose this particular fetus and the person who grows up under these conditions find themselves with what you call a dual personality. With proper care, one or the other can be dismissed from this human vehicle or human expression and the other one must seek out another fetus for it's expression.

From that point on, you absorb the necessary minerals and food elements which cause your physical to develop. It isn't by accident that your physical goes through various stages as it is born within the womb. It is through the normal development of thought patterns that these things come about. You absorb the natural minerals and vitamins from the mother and it is her responsibility to consume the proper foods so that they can be transferred to this living being that is being fostered by her. If she does not eat the proper foods, this body or fetus does not develop as it should and sometimes at the time of birth there are serious deficiencies materially and sometimes the material offspring does not recover from these initial deficiencies; but generally they do. Even at early childhood, the individual has certain cravings for certain foods and the parents aren't always aware that these cravings are extremely important to their child. They ignore them and they say to their child, 'this is what is good for you because we feel so.' But your instinct, if you wish to call it that, or your spirit body knows it's deficiencies and tells your material body to cry out for these deficiencies, to be fulfilled so that your physical can grow normally. As one grows older, one has more control over the consumption of foods and therefore, the responsibility transfers from the parents to the child and ultimately completely to the child.

Now, the aging process in very interesting. You say you mature in your late teens and this is true for at that time your mental image of yourself has fulfilled it's creation; you have created that which you see. That which you view in the mirror is the figment of your thinking. You put every cell exactly where it is because of the mental image you created for yourself. Understand this thoroughly and you will understand yourself.

Your body is continually growing, continually replacing cells. Millions of cells a day are being disposed of and new cells created every minute of every hour of every day. The aging process may surprise you. The aging process is brought about by lack of proper exercise. It is brought about by lack of meditation in one's vibratory pattern. As you grow into childhood, generally at the age of from 8 to 15 years, your spiritual self has generally fulfilled it's mission in creating a physical body which is acceptable in it's own eyes. It has not, at this time, learned to fear, to become anxious, all of which are poison to your system. As you go into later youth, you cease to exercise regularly and your exercises become more sedate. It is not becoming of the individual to play heartily when he is a grown person or she is a young lady. Now, this is man's standards which he set for himself. If you were to exercise as you exercised as a child in your teens and if you could relax as completely and divorce yourself from fretting, worrying and fear, you could live physically for as long as 900 years. This is your prerogative. Each one of these cells that is being built in your system daily requires certain minerals, salts, acids and carbon to build itself. It is your responsibility to this physical to provide these elements which are necessary for your body matter to create healthy, vibrant new cells. You see, with your body continually renewing itself, you can have eternal youth, This is a fact. This is a law. You must learn firmly that you create the conditions either by neglect or by concern which cause the disharmony of the functioning of your physical.

There is no so called disease in your physical which cannot be overcome with proper spiritual vision. There is a condition which can be created whereby the cells in your body which are being rejected or are being expended, are not being removed from your system because of damage to various organs and these expended cells form small pockets in your system; they become a foreign element to your normal body's protective system. Your body's protective system attacks these cells which are now foreign to the system the same as it would a virus or any other foreign element in the system. These protective cells consume these foreign bodies which were formerly part of your physical functioning abnormally and leave a residue like carbon. That is why with an x-ray this condition is readily noticeable in the film which you use. This residue becomes hard; hard as a coal or a clinker, as you might call it, in a fire. This hard condition is not the growth itself but it is the deposit of the results of these foreign elements being consumed. You call this condition a cancerous growth. It is caused by inadequate circulatory conditions; improper elimination of the foreign matter of the system. For every one of these cells, upon it's ceasing to be useful to your system at the time it is separated and replaced by a new cell, is a foreign element in the system and it gets into your digestive tract and it is mixed with your waste and it is eliminated from your system. So, your blood vessels, as you call them, are quite essential to distributing food to the new cells and more than this, your veins are important to remove these expended cells and transfer this expended material to your kidneys which absorb these dead cells. You might wish to call them dead cells but we wish to call them foreign elements, for there still is a certain amount of life in these at the time they are expended. These cells are separated by your kidneys and are expelled from your system. Therefore, it is very important to your body construction and maintenance that you get proper exercise to keep the blood flowing violently, thoroughly through your whole system. Cause yourself to have the proper relaxed attitude for when you become excited or have a continuity to negative thought, your thought is reflected somewhere in your physical and you deny your physical organs or area of expression, the proper blood flow in and away from this particular area and consequently inflammations will be caused. Irritations will develop by the toxins which doctors call the poisons created by these cells which are not properly transferred form the area. They become a toxin to the system and these generate what you call an inflammation; an irritation and this is the birth of what you call disease.

What we are saying is, you can create and you can eliminate these conditions. You may not eliminate the sore that the residue leaves but like a pearl you can coat this condition; this residue condition with a shell which will isolate it from the sound tissue and cause it to be dormant or inert. Because it is not the cinder that is damaging; the cinder is merely the result of the damaging condition. This is why one can, in a matter of weeks and months, consume oneself by allowing this condition to compound itself by lack of exercise and diet. There is not an individual who has this condition in their system who cannot, with the proper attitude, diet and therapeutic treatment of their system, overcome this condition or cause a 'reverse cycle.'

It is desirable to drink liquids and eliminate any and all sedation from the system. You must have conditions in your system which will cause you to relax for it is the frustrations basically which cause this condition initially. You must be forced to exercise, for you must flush this condition from the system and the only way you can get your blood to flow is by violent exercise. Now, I am not saying that you have to run a mile a day for you can run in one spot. You can do your work with vigor; anything that will get the blood boiling will be quite useful.

One must remove all sedation from their diet for it is sedation that causes the functions of your normal organs to slow down and this is quite contrary to the needs of the moment, for these organs must be functioning not at a slower pace but at an abnormal pace to overcome this condition. Then they must realize they have improper dietary conditions which cause these accumulations to come about. Vitamin E is extremely essential in treatment, for vitamin E, as you call it, allows your veins and arteries to remain pliable and absorbent. You must have your complete complex of B vitamins, especially B6 and B12 are extremely important to a person exposed to this condition. You never can take too much Vitamin C and this is extremely essential to the well being of your physical. There are those who say you can take excessive amounts of Vitamin E and C but they are erroneous in their thinking. There is an oil base being used for the ingress of vitamins in your system which is generally detrimental or acts as a foreign element in your system. Your body reacts to this oil, not to the vitamin that is being carried within it. It is best to use natural vitamins or vitamins not in an oil base.

Speaking of oil, there is one other oil I wish to bring to your attention. Vitamin F, as you call it, is not normally known as Vitamin F but is the unsaturated oils in vegetables and grain. Some use safflower oil for this purpose. Now, it is this oil that you eliminate and discard from the food that you eat by your refining process. But it is this very oil which God gave you as being the staff of life. When they speak of grain as being the staff of life, they are referring to the oil that is in this grain which is the oil upon which all of your organs rely on for their nutrients. It is through this oil that your joints lubricate themselves and that all of your organs in your body function. It is through these oils that the various chemicals in your body amalgamate and transfer to your various functions. When you deny your physical body these oils, these various functions are caused to become eliminated or diminished and you have what you call deficiency diseases. Most people have a deficiency disease of one manner or another because they have refined these essential oils from their cooking.

It is essential that you consume much of this oil in your daily diet. With this you will have eternal youth for this is the youth vitamin that was given to you by God's law at the beginning but you have grown away from God's law. Now we know you are returning to God's law for there is a great revolution in the making throughout your whole known world which will amalgamate all mankind as predicted and a great renaissance of intelligence as to the essential elements of life.

Chapter 16

Forms of Life

JESUS OF NAZARETH lived by the laws and dared to tell the common people secrets which were kept by the Priest's and the Rabbi's. They practice these laws improperly to gain control over the people to enslave the populace. Jesus of Nazareth taught these laws in a manner in which the populace could understand them and He taught that these laws would free them of all material restriction so they could expand their avenues of expression and have unlimited access to powers which were so diligently concealed by the priesthood. Once you have overcome your material limitations, you can expand beyond your wildest imaginative scope. These laws which were demonstrated, are not super natural laws. These are laws which are natural—God's laws.

Man deviated from these laws because he became concerned over self and wished to indulge these laws for his own benefit and this is sin—the opposite of love. Sin is self-centeredness; personal motivation. Love is the expansion of self; the losing of oneself. And when one is overwhelmed by love their countenance is not limited to their own immediate environment. For love, like a pebble in water, causes rings to expand ever and ever larger.

This is the law. Your motivation is the basis of life. The reason you perform an act is what is important. The act in itself is the same in many instances but the recipient of this act, very often, is not cognizant of whether this act is performed in love or lust or sin. So therefore, you must examine your motive before you perform an act. It is the motive that determines whether you are living by God's law or man's law.

We spoke of conception; we spoke of creation; we spoke of various forms of life being compatible to the area in which they exist. The same thought pattern on many spheres of influence manifests itself in the manner which is common to that area. If an earthling, as you are called by your people, a Christ child as you are called by our people, were to go to another planet which is under another spirit control, you would manifest of that planet, not as you manifest on this planet but in the form of life which is common to that planet. Now, there have been many references in your publications of unexplained entities entering your realm of influence from outer space, as you call it, as being figments of the imagination of the parties who claim they saw these objects but this is in error for these people who see these objects see this form at a distance.

There are those on your planet who vibrate to a plane sufficiently high that they can tune into these entities and converse with them but they are not unlike you in spirit; only in physical form. If they were to remain in this atmosphere for a period of time long enough for their thought patterns to adjust to your environment, they would manifest as you manifest. There are those among you who have done just this; who have come from other spirit influences or spiritual realms and are among you at this moment. They have been dispersed throughout your known world, as you call it, and the number is increasing daily.

Now, these are coming not to invade or to take over or destroy that which you have and hold so dear. They have been sent here to fulfill and I wish to emphasize the word 'fulfill', the prophesy of Jesus of Nazareth.

You all have, in previous incarnations, been on many different planets not just this one. There are certain chosen ones who are manifesting throughout your world at this moment to set the tempo of the thought patterns of the populace in general so that they may become receptive to this great overwhelming love-force which will transcend all materialism in the not too distant future. The time is at hand for this manifestation. I can assure you this will be so.

There will be many of the so-called chosen ones who will be put in influential positions in industry and politics to bring this about. This is a careful evolvement of mass psychology. Mankind has been taught a lesson of the futility of lust and apathy, for it is through these avenues of thought that all crime is committed. Man has strayed from the purity of purpose; is being reborn in spirit and once again will recognize the importance of spirit in his thinking. He has deviated greatly from the truth and from the light of all life. He will, in the not too distant future, find himself; I am speaking of mankind in general, and will cause himself to either be reborn in spirit or be obliterated by spirit, for when the entity has been dissipated there is no energy destroyed. The great love-force will bombard this sinful thought pattern and will disperse it and the spirit of the entity will be absorbed by the great love-force. Ultimately, all will be consumed and man will live in peace and unison. This may surprise you but it will be so because we have spoken in the past that there is no death. It is true. I use the word death because it is a term which you understand; there is merely a changing of status of the elements of thought or the elements of matter which is the result of thought but there is no destruction of spirit or matter. You can only disperse, not destroy so therefore, there is no death.

Anyone who chooses to live outside of love will suffer the consequences materially and physically for they are in violation of the law of love. They create a disharmony within their being and this disharmony reflects in physical conditions which are not tolerable. You may inadvertently, through thought patterns, create conditions which adversely affect you and not be aware that through your ignorance you are sending out discordant thought patterns. These can be recognized and corrected if you will but overcome self concern.

There is nothing in life that is insurmountable. There is nothing in life that is miraculous. All law, all spiritual law, to be more specific, is normal law not supernatural.

'To thine own self be true.' You must remember that since you are part of God thought is also part of God. Thought is part of the Christ spirit and is visible to all that is spiritual. You cannot hide your thoughts from those around and about you for there is no darkness which can conceal them, no light which can obliterate them. The only reality is thought. Everything around and about you, including yourself, is a manifestation of thought and to us thought is life. There are those who are able to tap what you call creative thinking. There are those who have learned, in previous incarnations, how to rise to this higher realm of thought and they relay it to you at you plane of thought.

Now, mankind in general rises in his thought pattern steadily from year to year. You must understand that the world and the law have been here since inception. Therefore, you merely discover or rise up to a level of thought and you touch this level of thinking and you manifest at that level. The level of attainment at present of the average man, exceeds the level at the time of Jesus of Nazareth. Therefore, the average intelligence has increased, for mankind in general has stepped up the ladder several rungs and he is worthy of the higher realm of thought and will benefit thereby. In meditation you must seek to raise your vibration to a higher plane of thought to release yourself from the limitations of a plane of thought in which you find yourself. This is what Jesus of Nazareth accomplished at will. It took him many, many years to lower His vibration to the level of man so that He could communicate.

When He was Moses He rose to a high level. When He was Isaiah He rose to a high level. When He was Khrisna He rose to a high level and I could speak of many more. This was the same entity which came back to cause mankind to understand once again the laws of God and finally the laws were demonstrated by this one. This electrifies man. These laws are simple laws. Know thyself and humble yourself in the knowledge that you are an essential part of the Christ Spirit.

Each one of you, through meditation, can attain the level of the realm within the Christ Spirit of Jesus of Nazareth. It is true that He was a high individual who came back to your plane of existence to show you by example the manner in which the law works and the futility of material, sinful thinking. When one understands the law of spirit, one can understand that flesh is nothing; that this flesh body can be disposed of; can be reactivated at the will of the spirit control.

There is nothing in the Bible that says that Jesus of Nazareth lost the spark of life, as you call it. on the cross. You must remember that this flesh body was taken from the cross and placed on a slab, covered with a cloth and there were no embalming fluids used. Knowing the power of spirit, it should not amaze you to know that with spirit power this slab or stone was rolled away from the door. The spirit of Jesus of Nazareth, as we know it, took control over this flesh and He walked from this cave and knowing that He had to conform to the entities around and about Him, He picked up clothing from a beggar who had been sleeping close by and walked up the road towards Jerusalem. When He had fulfilled His mission in Jerusalem, He went elsewhere in your planet and manifested in a similar manner. You must understand that when one is spirit and one has complete control over their physical, they can by mental force, mental control, raise or lower the vibration level of the physical and cause it to dissolve or dissipate as pure thought and re-appear elsewhere by dropping the vibration lower and lower to a new fresh entity. Jesus of Nazareth could do this in an instant for He knew God's law and He did just this. And I will confirm the various stories, as you may call them, that this same spirit entity manifested itself on every continent. He did manifest the tablets. It was through His Moses countenance that He caused these tablets which were destroyed in the Near East, to be re-written again and deposited in the hills in this general vicinity, for here again, He deposited tablets in what you call Central America.

He deposited tablets also at Mecca and there are still many scrolls which have not been re-discovered which will be discovered in the not too distant future once this turmoil is over and through an inadvertent act of man caused by his selfish desire, he will uncover more scrolls for the benefit of mankind in general.

Chapter 17

Creating a Symphony

LIFE IS A vibration. Light is vibration. Music is vibration. Heat is vibration. Flesh is the result of vibration.

That which holds the vibration in continuity, as you call it, is electricity and magnetism. A fine musical composition is harmonic vibration. You are a symphony. When you cause a discordant note it becomes readily identifiable in a malfunction of your physical and until you re-harmonize this tone quality it's discordant condition will remain.

When we cause the great love force, the God force or cosmic ray, whichever word you wish to use to overwhelm the individual and cause a re-alignment of the vibration pattern or your symphony and eliminate the discordant note, you are then made whole as a symphony which would be composed from our plane of existence. Each of you has their own symphony and that is why your physical temple is different one from the other.

Now, you have the capability of changing bars in this symphony to change your outward appearance. You have been as you call it, with a certain symphonic composition. This has been placed in your environment as part of an overall vibration pattern. Each chord is essential to each successive chord formed in a musical bar.

There are individuals who will attract to themselves various prophets. These prophets who are attracted to them as individuals were of the same vibratory pattern when they were on the earth plane. You must not be disturbed by the fact that various prophets in this form of existence choose different vehicles to express themselves for there is a compatibility of vibration and no relationship between your sincerity and those who you attract for like attracts like.

As you go up the ladder, you will add to your band and you will drop from your band. There is continual progression. Those who do not progress will find themselves going around aimlessly and when the overwhelming symphony is ultimately composed or re-discovered, the wheat will be separated from the chaff and the chaff will be consumed in the fire.

The reason we use the expression of fire is symbolic, for fire in your understanding, burns or destroys that which you consider consumed. Now, you of greater intelligence know that that which is consumed is merely transferred to different elements; into different forms of living matter and is absorbed by the general pool of elements and re-assigned to those who are harmonious. This is the only approach we have of cleansing your earth image of sin. Ultimately, this fire (understand this is symbolic) will consume the disharmony of your plane of existence. There will be a time in the for-seeable future, (when I mention for-seeable future, I am speaking of within the present limitations of your existing temples or bodies), when there will be a falling off of the so-called religious concept and then there will be a resurgence; a power resurgence which will overwhelm and you will have a birth of the Christ Spirit in those who remain. Many will pass on mysteriously. —Do not be alarmed, there is no death.

Those of you who are chosen, because you have chosen yourselves, will be strengthened because you will be absorbing this energy from those who are dissipated. Your form of appearance will deviate slightly. You will find that your physical will generally be more slender than it is; your brain capacity or your heads will tend to be greater in size and your impression in your forehead will be more pronounced. Other than that your physical will not deviate.

You may ask yourself why disharmony entered into symphonies? You must remember that for every force there is a complementary and opposing force or a balancing effect. It is when these two forces are not balanced that one tends to overpower the other; not completely but in various areas temporarily. It is essential at all times that we have all of these forces. Otherwise there would be chaos. Therefore, we wish that each of you, individually, would seriously meditate daily. Open yourself up to the higher realm without fear in your hearts and we will at this time place your being in perfect balance. This you must practice daily for this if essential to your progression. We do not wish you to lose your individuality, we only wish that you do not distort your individuality from that which was given to your temple that you chose upon returning to your phase of expression. You must cherish this temple. You must care for this temple.

Those of you who wish to contact the higher realm must practice. We do not ask you to deny yourself of so-called rewards. We ask you to be pure in your intent and have faith and you will do no harm. We are only interested in creating a harmonious atmosphere to bathe the individuals. When we speak of fear we do not mean the common interpretation of being afraid or being punished. We like to think of fear as being an emotion whereby the individual does not wish to displease the loved one who is looking over them on our plane. This fear is love. We do not wish to injure; we do not wish to cause a disharmonious condition around or between you and this higher plane. Once you understand fear, you understand love because fear and love are of common use. This may sound paradoxical but it is basic.

As I expressed once, the purpose of your actions are what we judge you by. There is another confusing element to you on your plane which I wish to clarify briefly, that is the element of time. We are living in the ever present on this plane. To you the cycle of the moon is a positive period of time as it is to us also. That which is of long duration to you is just a moment to us. Therefore, when we say soon, it could be many, many moons to our division at this close level. Understand this and you will not be as confused concerning timing.

When we speak of elements or seasons on time, we very rarely speak in terms of which period of time. We only know at which point in the cycle an event will transpire. This we are positive of but we do not know whether it is the first, second, third, forth or subsequent cycle of the twelve cycles or moons. Remember this well for this is the cause of many misinterpretations in your limitations.

Chapter 18

The Individual

I WISH TO delve more thoroughly into individual personality. Each of you as I stated once before, is a symphony. That is the reason certain parts of your body function as they do. When you sustain a physical injury, the replacement tissue which was destroyed accidentally is replaced precisely in the same state as it was when destroyed. Doesn't it seem strange to you that every part of your body is self healing, that every part of your body replaces itself generally once every seven years? Every cell you have at this moment you did not have seven years ago and you will not have seven years from now. The body as it exists now will be completely replaced. By the same token if you, by will or by acceptance, change the score of your symphony, you change continuously for a sufficient length of time to allow your cellular structure to adjust itself to bring about the visual manifestation of this revision in your musical score.

I may be oversimplifying this but I do wish to have you understand thoroughly that you do have complete control over this physical temple. You can cause a complete cure of any physical condition within a period of time. The only deterrent to proper visual control is what you would call a discordant note; an electrician would call it static for you are vibration. Every element in your environment is vibration. It is the harmonics of the individual; the combination of tone as you might call it, that causes the physical manifestation as you see it. Even the so-called inanimate objects are vibrating around you continuously and they will continue to vibrate unless some foreign element distorts their harmony of motion.

So when you give a healing, if you would ask the great love force you call God to re-harmonize the individual you would be more aptly placing emphasis at the proper level. For when you remove the discordant note or interfering vibration which ever you prefer, you cause the initial harmonious melody or symphony to play, in effect, a healing.

Most individuals bring on their illnesses through mistrust of themselves. They do not wish to admit it to themselves but they mistake a basic emotion. It is true that the individual is not sufficient unto himself to achieve all that he wishes to achieve. He must be humble and in his humbleness he will attain perfect unison with the grand symphony. Most individuals are aware of their limitations but they do not seem to be aware that they are a part of a great force; that they can assert this great force at any given moment. Most individuals are involved with ego and pride; they do not overcome this; they do not learn the lesson of being part of a great force. They look to themselves individually. They know of their inadequacy and this frustration; this discordant attitude, causes various distortions within your symphony causing distortion in various organs within your temple and subsequent damage to the physical manifestation within the individual. When one learns to live in harmony; live in peace; live in assurance that one can attain by losing themselves in a great symphony, they not only have their limited beauty of melody but also a beautiful basic music of all life. This is ever available but one must attain an attitude of feeling secure and not allowing fear or anxiety to enter, for this is the devil, as you call it. Fear and anxiety are the cause of all distortion. Very often it is triggered by vanity, ego and lust.

Once you maintain your composure and this word composure is properly constituted, it is as the composer composes. So, if you maintain your composure, you maintain perfect health and you are able to disseminate any problem which is placed before you and have complete control over the situation at hand. As you work closer with this great symphony, you become less and less emotionally involved with your problems; you will look at them with an indifference and when you look at them with an indifference, you see them as they really are. You are devoid of the emotional trap of entanglement with your problem. It is these emotional entanglements which cause basic destruction of your symphony. When one can gear their mind as you call it, to this level or this plateau, you will find that you will have a life that runs so smoothly you will accomplish ends which are way beyond where you place your imaginary limits. The only limitation an individual has is that which he places upon himself.

You can tap this great force not by willing it to happen but by creating conditions within yourself which will attract it to you and have it flow through you. You must shut off your awareness, your pride, your ego and stand to the side and watch this great force flow through you at your direction. This is why some of you hear beautiful music as you pass or you arise or ascend to a higher plane of existence, for you are hearing the tune which you will be bathed in, in the future. You are beautiful music. Each of you is a beautiful melody. Each of you is a different melody.

It is not by accident that you are here, for the angel world does have a governing group who watches carefully over the advancement of man. As they see fit, they cause changes in the general crescendo and also cause the tools to suit the plane of existence they wish to have mankind ascend to.

It is not by accident that men were born fifty years ago to perform acts which are not even vaguely in the minds of men at the time of their birth. What I am saying is that each of you, on the face of your goal has been placed here with a mission. You are all part of the great symphony. You are all an essential part of this great symphony and if you do not function in this capacity you find yourself frustrated. You are aware of the fact that you are in discord and do not know how to correct it because man hasn't realized until now that he is part of a great mass of energy. Once one discovers his mission and changes to that mission, he grows and finds happiness within that great mission.

You must understand that the Great Counsel looks down upon you in light of the full symphony. One of you may be a violin by comparison; another may be an oboe and another a horn and when you are all playing your instrument properly we have a beautiful, beautiful sound. You must also understand that when this Great Counsel looks down, that you are not unlike ants in an ant hill and if an individual by accident or otherwise sees fit to eliminate himself from the symphony, we must replace this one with another who will carry on. This may sound like an indifferent attitude toward individual life but to us we must maintain the symphony for progression and any individual who does not co-operate creates a condition which is intolerable and thus eliminate themselves. This is quite possible. It is not God's will as some people say, when an individual passes on. It is the result of their will. They violated the law inadvertently or purposely it makes no difference. The law was violated and they pay the penalty. So you must understand the nature of our position. The whole picture must be maintained at all times. This is essential for the progression of all mankind.

You create the conditions around and about you through ignorance; we call it sin. That is why it is well for you to take an indifferent approach; a third-party approach I think is more understandable to your way of thinking, on all problems; on all facets of your life and you will be less apt to violate the law.

We wish that you have deep emotion. We do not wish that you be emotionless for it is these deep emotions that cause your symphony to have sparkle, life and beauty. We only wish that you do not distort this beautiful melody with fear. We must not cater to individuals, You each have a mission and if you do not fulfill this mission, we will find another who will fulfill it; for any mission is greater than the individual.

Remember, you are born in harmony; you are a perfect being when you are born; you are a perfect being when you take over an embryo. You are the one that causes this embryo to take the shape that it takes. As a child, you do not speak as readily, walk as readily; see or hear as readily because your physical being is not fully mature. Now, this may be strange to your way of thinking but if a child was allowed in an environment devoid of an education, as you call it, and the spirit that was placed in this embryo was allowed to manifest the intelligence would not be different; the intelligence would be as we gave it. It would not be distorted and disillusioned by the twisted, distorted thoughts of the accumulation of knowledge created by man, I am saying that the intelligence you have today you had at birth.

I do not wish to cause you to misunderstand life. You are part of the great Spirit Force; an essential part. I deeply beseech each of you to bask in this great force as you would bask in the sunshine. Absorb this great energy; fulfill your missions; live in the great love; manifest the great love through harmonious approach and live in the shelter of the Great I Am.

Chapter 19

Neptune

ON OUR PLANET Neptune, we do not have the ambient temperature that you have on your planet. Our atmosphere is relatively light by comparison to yours so we derive our heat and our atmosphere by means of chemical reaction with basic elements within the crust of our planet. Your civilization has just recently been introduced to this energy that is derived from the earth soil on which you walk. This gradually becomes united with chemicals in the atmosphere and in the process creates heat and energy. We tap this energy by illumination and power. We have learned to take this same energy and use it for motivation purposes.

This force is basic. The only reason you are not progressing faster with this force is that you fear it. The radiation from this force is the power we use for motivation and you are trying to shield yourself from this great force. What we do on this plane is channel this great force and direct it as you would a missile. We have a small power cell which we attach to our waistband and we merely activate this device and we can travel at will without supplementary vehicles to our point of destination.

Many of you on your plane of existence have been concerned for the possibility of invading, as you call it, from outer space. To us this is amusing for it is because of outer space life structures that you exist. You progress from this plane of existence. It is true that the Christ Spirit is the Master of this plane but we have our Master also. We do not involve ourselves with fear and mistrust. When you elevate yourself from your present plane of existence many of you will ascend to our realm for a while.

We see fit from time to time to form a group of many entities and we energize our power pack and descend in a group to your planet and we are seen at times as a shiny mass. There are occasions when we have encountered an individual who is on a plane of consciousness which is approaching our plane of consciousness and we converse with this one. We can come and go in an instant and we do so. You see, we have learned to control our emotions and we have learned to raise or lower our vibration at will. This is what you wish to accomplish. This Christ Spirit will manifest itself again within a decade and you will be over whelmed by this higher vibration.

There will be a period; a brief period when many of you will be exhilarated and many will be overcome with fear and anxiety and you will be separated in this manner and the ones who are consumed with fear will destroy each other, This may amaze you, but it is a law that you are consumed by your own thoughts. It is well that you understand this basic truth, that you control your destiny by the thoughts you create. You are constantly creating thoughts;

creating images. Do not lose sight of this fact that the only real thing there is, is thought and everything else is a manifestation of thought. Learn this well and you will ascend at will.

We travel on vibration. We set a focal thought; an intense image as to where we want to go and concentrate on this image and a path is established for us and we merely follow this pattern that is set up. We could travel almost instantaneously from our abode to your abode and you can do likewise. There are many forms of life not merely the flesh life. We are not as restricted in our activities as you are and you will gradually elevate to a higher plane of activity. If you learn to project thought, you can travel on this thought if you purify this thought. What I am saying is, do not have any doubts; do not have any diversions where this thought is concerned. When you learn not to dilute your thought you can travel as we travel. You can disintegrate your lower vibration body and you can rebuild the same body elsewhere. You are capable of leaving your physical body that you are embodied in now, travel to our planet and build your body again when you have completed your mission; you can dissolve this entity and travel back to the comfort of your temple where you left it reclining. This is a fact. This is as many of the Masters in the past have done.

Chapter 20

Other Planetary Influences

MAN WILL DISCOVER that there is an abundance of life on the planet Mars. Mars is one of the stepping off points; one of the marshalling points; one of the control points of life in general. They will discover that this so-called dust cloud that surrounds this planet is not in reality dust as you know it but an electronic screen which protects life on that planet from any outward disturbances from the higher plane and negative disturbances from the lower plane. It is from this area of influence that Earth assignments are consummated. So when you jokingly speak of the man on Mars, whether you know it or not, you are speaking the truth. Each one throughout your universe has come from Mars. Mars is a stage of existence that one enters into just prior to entering the realm you call Earth. Mars is not exclusively the planet of life. Venus they will discover has life; Saturn they will discover has life and the planet you call Pluto has the highest form of life in your universe.

When you see Saturn you see what is equivalent to a rainbow. They have mentioned this but they do not understand what causes this rainbow. Saturn is the area where all the spirit forces go when they pass from your plane of existence. There are some that go to this planet and contribute to the vibration patterns which emanate in your spectrum of colors. Now, this is the clearing house for all spirit entities when they first pass from your realm of existence. There are those who become absorbed in this great mass of energy vibration and there are those who go to this area of influence and absorb their deficiencies from those who have become dissipated, then they progress on. This will explain why there have been so many births as you call them, why some spirit entities never return and why the spirit world is never overcrowded. This is the manner in which we progress en-masse.

We go from Saturn to Neptune; from Neptune to Venus; from Venus to Mars;; from Mars to the Moon and from the Moon back to your condition. There are a few steps in between but these are essentially the primary points of contact. Each of these areas has influence in your progression and the clarification of your soul and it is quite true that Venus is the area where you absorb the love forces prior to your progression either to Pluto or to Mars depending on which avenue of expression is important to the Great I Am at the time.

We now have taken a spirit entity and to use your language, we have purified and clarified this entity. However, if this entity wishes to develop further and he discovers, or it discovers, which is more nearly a correct term; for there is no male or female entity in this realm; that in order to progress one must experience emotional conditions. The only plane in which emotions can be experienced is your plane of existence. Call it a school if you wish but you must experience deep emotional conflict in order to gain what you call wisdom or insight.

Each and every object on your plane of existence goes through the same process because there are those among you at this moment who wonder about the function of the other planets and planetary areas in your universe. You see, there are vegetable matter realms and animal matter realms in your universe also and they have their own areas the same as your human existence. This explains the other functions of the other planets. Now this may cause you to understand the various influences on your life; the various planetary positions at the time of your birth; for each of these areas of influence radiate and having existed on these various planets, you are attuned to the vibratory rates of each of these planets. As each of these planets come to an influential area, you tune in more readily with a certain planet or a combination of planets. Mankind has realized from the beginning of your recorded time that planetary influences are a reality and this is so, depending on your type of personality as to which planets influence which individuals at any given moment. We know this and man from the inception of recorded time has studied these trends and has evolved what he thinks to be, from scientific data, the influences which control the loves of individuals. This is not correct. You merely tune in to these various vibratory influences to replenish energies which at times are dissipated through erroneous actions and you require these little reminders, for these are the areas of the food for your souls. This is the food that Jesus of Nazareth spoke of; this is the cup of which He drank.

You will find that if you examine the scriptures carefully that there are only certain periods of the year when He preached and healed. For when He healed, He evoked the forces of the planet Saturn into the individual for this is the source of energy which is used as a battery to replenish that which an individual, through indulgence or improper levels of activity, causes the spiritual entity to be depleted. This is the source of the energy which you tap when you invoke the great healing force. You make direct contact with this source; this pool of energy and transfer it to serve the needs of the individual before you.

When there is need for an individual to come into material existence, this spirit entity, under the guidance of the power, is attracted to a contagion of inception which is inspired by the higher elements and we select the moment of inception. There are no accidental inceptions. Material beings may be disturbed or embarrassed but we select the moment; we select the bodies which the individual wished to dwell in to gain the experience to further strengthen; further solidify the individual entities. This may take your so-called romance and distort it but then again it may cause you to realize the reasons for the difference in personalities of the individuals that you erroneously feel you conceived. These are gifts to you. Like most gifts you either enjoy them you are distressed by them or you are not happy with them and set them aside. The fact of the matter is that we have seen fit to place a spirit entity into this condition. A woman could be the vehicle of any number of children and have every one a definite, distinctly different individual.

Now we very carefully select parents, as you call them, that would be compatible with the environment which we choose for the individuals to gain their experience. That is why there is always some trait of the parents in the off-spring. It is only because there is a similarity and they were chosen to be the vehicle through which the spirit force could manifest itself.

Jesus of Nazareth was born the same as any one else but the woman we chose was an exceptionally pure being. Her emotional elevation was on a high plane of existence and her husband was a church elder who was quite deeply involved in spiritual elements of his work. It is very difficult to find a combination such as this and when we saw this rare condition we took advantage of it and placed this spirit of high intensity in this womb. This may make some of you feel relieved, then it may disturb other humans for you will say to yourselves that this spirit told us that we, or you, depending on your point of view, are all born equal and now you tell us that this one was an exception. So therefore, you do not have to place the effort into your ascension for your destiny does not allow you to do so for you could not attain this level of existence. This is not true. The only difference is that this one was advanced at the time of inception and he advanced further. Any individual can advance to this same level if they would. I wish to repeat—ANY individual has the opportunity and the availability of all the same forces if they would but take advantage of them. You see, this one spirit entity has dedicated itself to the advancement of mankind in general and comes back periodically to inspire those around and about Him to greater heights of attainment. The only reason you are on this plane is to gain emotional growth. Emotional growth is like putting a piece of metal in a flame and heating it up to a higher rate of vibration and tempering it through experiences to a stronger state of existence.

Life, as you call it, is eternal. This is true but you must realize at this moment when we speak of life, we speak of life in general; that the individual entity, as an entity, does not necessarily remain as an entity in the eternal. If we see fit to dissipate this entity and regroup it we will do so. Naturally, we select what we consider the best and cause it to cycle through and then come back. There are many who seek to come back but do not come back for quite some time for we have no need of their condition in your plane of existence and we use them elsewhere. This is life. A basic understanding of life.

Chapter 21

You Must Overcome

MATERIAL LAW GENERALLY concerns itself with possession and ego. Spirit law overcomes these two basic sins. With spirit law, you are pleased to become part of the great whole; become a part of the great Christ Spirit. You glory in it and manifest; and even though your manifestations take on materialistic aspects to materialistic people around and about you, the motivating force is spiritual in nature. Put first things first and all will be given unto you. This is a fact which the Great I Am considers the ultimate in progression. This overcomes the emotions which cause fear and anxiety which are the basic causes of conflict. In spiritual thinking, you are secure in this great force, for there is no need to fear or be anxious for your future while you are basking in the light of your Father's love.

There are those who do not overcome ego but this is an emotion which must be overcome to make the final step to a higher existence. The higher existence is not remote existence but one that anyone can attain if they would apply themselves and overcome ego. This is the greatest stumbling block in the path of progress, for this is the phase that becomes utmost in the minds of those who have tapped a limited level of the spirit power. They bask in the notoriety and attention that they receive from their fellowman when they can demonstrate their ability to contact the higher realm. They get glimpses of the higher realm but they limit their progress to a certain level and until they overcome this emotion, they will remain at this level and will not progress. They will become extremely frustrated. For it is like an individual on your physical plane being in a pool of water and anticipating drowning and reaching our for a branch that is within finger-touch reach and just being able to touch it on occasion and not being able to grab or cling to that which they know is security. One must overcome awareness of self to progress and do great works. One must loose themselves in the needs of all, then they will progress to the higher level of existence.

The people who do not find themselves in this plane of thought, find it difficult to witness the activity of the one who has been so blessed, for they are concerned for this expended energy which this one is dissipating for the benefit of those around and about this individual and concerned about the depletion of energy within this individual. They do not realize that the energy that is being dispensed at this given moment or any given moment, is merely a transfer of energy which originates from our plane of existence to the individual who has been chosen to be the recipient of this energy. You see, the great sin is more concern for self than the needs of others. This is the greatest sin of all.

Know that you are a messenger; an essential messenger or medium through which a great force flows. You must be convinced in your mind of this and not be concerned for your individual convenience or inconvenience at the moment. You place yourself in the position of service and allow this great force to flow through you for the benefit of others. It is a sensation which you all desire but few attain. Everyone, as I said before, is capable of attaining this level of existence. You are also capable of ascending to the level that Jesus of Nazareth and five of His disciples and many prophets before Him had attained.

You sacrifice nothing by giving of yourself to a part of a great force. Do not cling to vanity; self awareness. Do not look to your individual capabilities but look to being lost in the white light. Look forward to being rather in the glories of the spirit force. Do not be concerned for material needs for these will be adequately provided for in proportion to your ability to lose yourself in the service of others. Do not lose yourself in your own power.

Those who have touched on the higher plane of existence find themselves quite distraught, nervous and anxious and thoughts do not become consistent in their being. It is like a static condition. They can overcome this; clarify this by loosing awareness of self; by loosing themselves once again in the needs of others and they will drop this condition and be free again to bask in the light. This is the trap that many cults fall into. They delve in communication with the great powers for personal glory and personal gain; personal advantage over others and consequently, they appear to advance as a meteor but because of their devious activities, like a meteor, they also descend and become dissipated. This is the reason why many of the Oriental philosophies and Indian philosophies on your continent have failed. You must understand that these philosophies are centered around the thought of personal advancement; personal edification; personal purification and personal gain. Many of these reach a level where they exploit these personal controls over the physical and demand admiration from their fellowman for the ability to control this physical at will but there lies their trap. Ego, as I said earlier, is a trap. It is the greatest of sins to overcome. Even though the greatest sin is apathy, ego is the root which causes apathy. Apathy is the result of self involvement; self awareness and self indulgence. When one overcomes this, one gains the world, as you call it and becomes complete master of that which is before him.

It may sound irregular to you, that in order to attain greatness you must loose yourself; loose your identity as an individual but this is true. You must place yourself in position to be an outlet for a great force and cause this great force to function as you would have it function with love and concern for others and then great things will be accomplished through you. This is in all the 'good books'. There is none good but God and He doeth the works. This is a simple straight forward statement. Allow yourself to be a channel; the avenue through which this great force can flow and there is no limit of your accomplishments; no limit whatsoever. Be grateful for the channel that you are for you have been constituted as individuals to be proficient in various phases on the over all symphony of existence and when you allow yourself to fall into your proper harmonic, you will be in position to allow your proportion of this great force to flow freely. Then you will not become disturbed by the ignorance of those around and about you but you will overcome and pray for their enlightenment.

You must remember that it is your place to overcome what you call human tendencies—we call them sin. Sin—you say you are born in sin—you are never born, you are created. Your birth is a result of choosing the embryo; call this birth if you will. You are born in an environment of sin not in sin. You absorb the environment or reject the environment of sin. It is not necessary that you live in sin for sin is a way of conduct. We wish that all mankind would overcome sin.

Now, you all dream; you all anticipate what you call Eden; others call it Heaven. This is not beyond your grasp because Heaven and Eden are just a materialistic or a spiritualistic expression used for peace and plenty with no concern for the needs of the individual. When you attach yourself to or when you attain the higher realm of existence, your attitude towards life is such that you are not concerned for your material needs for you know beyond a shadow of a doubt that these will be cared for. This is Eden and this is Heaven. You become quite sensitive to those around and about you and at times you become quite disturbed by their ignorance of the great laws but you overcome—you overcome. You have heard the expression of 'heaven on earth' and 'hell on earth'. These are merely planes of consciousness or levels of attainment. We have these forces of every nature available to us at all times. It is merely our prerogative as to when and which one we invoke for those around and about us. We allow the force to flow through us in proportion to the strength of our motivating power. The individual has control of this aspect. It can be as a trickle or it can be as a roaring, churning wave. These powers are available to any individual.

Chapter 22

Utilization of The Cosmic Forces

WE WILL SPEAK concerning the well being of the soul or of the entity as it manifests in human form. Through healing you are restoring the harmonic balance of the entity. You are merely the avenue of expression through which flows the river of thought patterns which has all avenues of expression contained within it. The body merely absorbs, from the material point of view, the necessary elements from this vast reservoir of thought power, that which is required to replenish that which has become distorted or depleted; restoring that initial balance within the system. The entity is to be the receiver of the food. For this is the food of which Jesus of Nazareth spoke. He also spoke of it as an analogy to water so that man could understand through illustration, that this energy is constantly flowing. This is the food of which He spoke.

The individual personality absorbs the energy or thought power which it requires for proper function. The healer or provider of the energy, is merely a vehicle through which this condition flows. The healer merely creates the proper atmosphere in which the depleted entity may find itself in the condition of restoration. This may sound vague but we are at a loss for proper verbiage at times in describing to you the rules of life as you understand them not as we know them. You are constantly bathed in the pool of energy. You become receptive and then you receive. You must, in order to drink of this food, place yourself in the attitude of expectancy and then, and only then, will you bring about the absorption of the proper harmonics which are normally oriented to the needs of what you call your soul. The only true food is this energy.

When one has thought energy being expanded, their is a triggering device within the system which switches off one's ability to absorb from this pool. Some refer to it as cosmic force; some call it the love force and some call it the God force. This is why the individual must, from time to time throughout the day, relax completely under conditions devoid of stress or strain so that one can, through complete relaxation, trigger this contact with the God force or the energy pool. This is the key to eternal life.

I am referring to eternal physical manifestation of a harmonious being. There is no such thing as a limit on longevity of physical manifestation of life, as you know it. One who is properly constituted emotionally, could live in an existence on your plane of expression; for hundreds of years. It is only the lack of ability to look outside one's self, in an atmosphere of serenity, that one can prolong one's material expression. The only condition which controls the so called aging process is not the fact that this energy is perpetual but the fact that one's attitude toward this aging process changes. You are oriented through error into believing and you accept this as natural law, that one must deplete normally in proportion to the time one exists on your plane of influence. This is not so. This is only because your fellowman has set up these erroneous conceptions that these apparent aging processes exist, for man does not necessarily age. If you could maintain the proper attitude and rise above the limitations that your fellow beings have placed upon you, you would not age but would retain the conditions of existence manifest at what you call the maturity level. There are no physical or material devices which can or will maintain physical well being.

Likewise, when we speak of food for the soul, we speak of food for the body. You are living and have available to you at all times, chemical and food elements which are required for the perfect well being of the material manifestation. It is essential that you have available at all times, the elements which have become depleted of emotional activity. Your spiritual being tells your material manifestation which chemicals it requires to replenish the depleted areas within the system.

Contrary to many theories, with a proper mental attitude, your physical being will not normally absorb chemicals into the system which are beyond the ability of the body to absorb. This is the quest that many have made when you speak of eternal life. They spoke of eternal physical manifestation of life. So, it is important that one remain calm for it is only when one overcomes anxiety and fear and self esteem, that one can readily place themselves into a pool of vital energy. Only in proportion to your ability to overcome these evils will you ascend to the proper state of existence.

As was expressed earlier, the purity of you desire is the key. I hope I have clarified a point which has caused many to seek the solution for mankind has missed the conditions of proper existence. I have tried to explain this from many points of view so that those who reap from many levels of existence will learn to partake of the food of life.

In summery, you are constantly bathed in a pool of energy which will not flow into your system until your attitude triggers the flow. Attitude! Attitude! Attitude! Attitude is the key word. In the process of having energy flow through any individual, one is exposed to the quantity of food in excess of their individual needs and this is the energy that maintains the health of the healer. Those who practice become an avenue or a flow of energy through which should slow the aging process tremendously within themselves. This is the greatest individual benefit derived from being a vehicle through which energy can flow to assist those around and about you. Therefore, if you wish, you may give of yourself freely, for in the process of giving of yourself freely you are not depleting yourself of energy which so many seen to be concerned about. On the contrary, you are bathed in a pool of energy which is of greater magnitude than those around and about you.

Now, to us on the spirit side of life, getting fat; I am speaking of spiritually fat; is desirable. If one lives a balanced existence with proper food energy, proper spirit energy, the physical manifestation will not become obese, as you call it. It is desirable that the individual allow as much spirit food or energy to pass through his vehicle as is possible because the more readily this energy flows through the individual, the more it strengthens and reinforces the personality of the true entity. To us this energy is as a ball of light and the more intense this ball of light becomes, the more readily it absorbs increased amounts of energy.

Each of you is a light; each of you is a star and we see you as stars and we gauge your value to us by the brightness and coloring of your star or light. This is the path of ascension. So it behooves you to serve others, for in serving others, you become exposed to greater amounts of this true energy of life and benefit thereby. You cannot possibly give too much energy away, as you think of it. This is impossible.

The sun is merely a high concentration of pulsating spirit entities. There are many suns as you know and there are many concentrations throughout the universe. There is a master force which controls and replenishes the energy absorbed by these suns, and in turn, these suns emit energy for the welfare of man and every object exposed to the rays of this great force or power.

Each sphere of influence has it's own general spirit force body which you, as individuals and every element of energy around and about you, are exposed to and a part of. We have an avenue where we can accelerate the aging process of the individual personally by depleting it from the spirit source of energy. We also have the ability of reversal of this process and rejuvenate with proper energy, so we do have the power of so-called life or death over the individual. We do not choose to exercise this because we know that any negative energy which we cause to flow through an entity will eventually be absorbed.

In your book you refer to as "The Bible", you speak of what you call the Holy Trinity and man has erroneously thought of this in terms of material manifestations. We speak of the Father (God power), the Son (who is the individual basking in this god power) and the Holy Ghost which is the mass of individuals forming the whole. You, at times, call this mass of energy which is the Holy Ghost; the Christ Spirit. Each of your planets absorbs it's energy from it's own individual sun. So the so-called trinity is a spiritual trinity. There is no reference to material expression whatsoever. When I speak of the Father, in direct translation, it is 'farther'; the farther-out control or the farther-out source of energy; the great master mind. I hope this clarifies this misconception.

When the Prophets say to you that a good deed is returned to you a thousand fold, they are not exaggerating, for as one opens oneself, they allow themselves to rise to a higher plane of awareness. Fear and anxieties are destructive forces. Replace them with calmness, serenity and confidence which is directness of action.

Chapter 23

Music as Food

WE HAVE ESTABLISHED that your physical being and your physical well-being is dependent on harmonics and that every organ; every member of the flesh is an individual harmonic. So actually, as we have stated once before, your physical is a symphony. Therefore, music is composed at the time of the conception and generally remains guiding this form of life. Any individual who wishes to destroy another individual can do so by creating a discordant atmosphere musically but by the same token one can take a discordant atmosphere and make it harmonious by playing the proper music. That is why certain people tend to certain types of music. You can tell the personality of an individual by the music he selects.

During the growing process, the individual's taste for music is basically a non-descriptive type of scoring. This is only because they are growing. The body requires many different harmonics. This will explain apparent aimless behavior or the non-directional behavior and by the same token, this is basically why, as you call it, 'birds of a feather stick together'. As one ages or matures the true harmonics will crystallize.

You can use music as a stimulant. Music can cause you to be sad, cause you to be happy or cause you to be vital. Look to the future refinement in music to create mass psychological reaction. You can take a whole nation, analyze their tendency to music and turn them from a peace loving people into a hostile type of people. This is why war music has a certain beat and why church music has a certain beat.

You can create any personality trait with controlled sound or harmonics. You can take a person who is mad by your standards and cure them of their madness by playing certain harmonics for exposing them to these harmonics, you allow them to unify or re-harmonize. There are instruments in existence today protected by government ownership, which can disintegrate various forms of life. Man knows of this. I don't know of any scientific approach in the world of sound but this must be accomplished. It is a vast field. This is the food that Jesus of Nazareth spoke of. This food is just as essential to one's well being as the material food placed in the system.

As a point of illustration: a teenaged child listens to music constantly for this is essential to growth. They use this music as food for it is this music that the body absorbs to grow on. That is why they use music incessantly; very much to your annoyance. They are absorbing necessary harmonics required by their system for growth. This may explain to you the mystery that most parents haven't solved yet as to why their children have to have so much noise around them. This explains also why when children play they release noises. This noise they release is a surplus of spent harmonics from their system.

We know that you can destroy a whole civilization with distortion of sound. In industry, it has been learned that with selections of familiar music, more productive labor is produced. You can create moods with sound injection. This subject is great in depth and is a future weapon. You will find that you associate different musical sounds with different atmospheres. Scenario writers for movie houses learned quite some time ago that when you play certain types of music, the individual is placed in a semi hypnotic state and listens in a certain mood and expects to see or hear certain things happen and are disappointed when they do not or are elated when they do. That is the reason for the re-birth of your soul music. Understand this thoroughly and you will have the greatest weapon or the greatest peace creating atmosphere. There is no tool; no vehicle of destruction as powerful as music by this control. Man has not until now, accepted music as a means of life. Music is food for the soul and that is why music is the international language—not language, but international food.

I know that what I have just given you is not simple to explain or absorb but it is profoundly correct. One who can control the sound of music can control the mood of the world.

Chapter 24

Faith

I WISH TO speak concerning individuality. Mankind is experimenting and they are becoming more mystified every day by the complete self-sustained condition of the human body. The body, as you know it, has it's own set of harmonics which causes your body to appear as it does and function as it does and if there are discordant elements introduced into the system the body immediately sets up anti-bodies which tend to eliminate or consume the invading disharmony whether it be a disturbing thought or emotion or a disturbing piece of flesh or a foreign object.

This is why there is much difficulty with implanting foreign organs into the body by what you call an operation. Unless there is a harmonic similar to the organ being replaced, the new organ will be consumed by the body because the harmonics know no flesh and they try to re-establish themselves. It is far better for the individual to correct their thinking or get involved in deep hypnosis to correct the condition and re-establish their harmonics so that the original organ can repair itself rather than to have a transplant. There is not an object in the body; a cell or an organ which when relieved of stress, will not automatically mend itself. This is a fact.

When you get involved in healing, if you would pray that the individual be harmonized; be overwhelmed by the great love force, you would be seeing the truth of the law, for in harmony there is proper function. It is this simple—no more, no less. Know this fact well.

Faith is the key to the door of contact. You need faith to contact us. You need faith to trigger a force for faith is the key that opens the door. Without faith there is no movement of energy. Unless there is movement of energy no progress with the individual or those around and about him is made. Remember, it is through implicit faith that Jesus of Nazareth contacted us and it was His faith alone; his intensity of faith, that caused a pure vehicle through which we could examine the individual and replace the depleted intensity of harmonics in the system.

Jesus did not do the works just as He said. He merely turned the key and allowed spirit to instantaneously examine the causes of the erroneous symptoms and correct them for the flesh responds in accordance with normal harmonics of the system. When you have raised to this level of faith, we will be able to flow through you as we did through Jesus.

Faith is the foundation of activity. That explains why so many do not receive. They do not have faith in themselves or in us (spirit). The instant the individual attains this faith the forces flow freely. We cannot generate faith. This may surprise you. We generate all other forces but we do not generate faith. Faith is the motive; faith is the key; faith is the cause of all activity which is spiritual. Once you have faith, the nonsense of the evil thoughts of those around and about you will amuse you because of their ignorance, for you will see them in their true light and rather than be disturbed by their acts of ignorance, you will see them as evil.

You see, there were many prophets who tried to define evil for mankind and mankind misinterpreted these great wisdoms and mankind become devious in twisting these truths to his convenience. Jesus of Nazareth came to demonstrate the law. He came to demonstrate the power which is available to the individual when they have overcome evil. This may surprise you but evil is necessary for there must always be a balancing force for the light and when they come into balance, to mankind in general, it goes in the direction of evil or light. The pendulum has turned now and the light or enlightenment will begin to prevail.

Evil is self-awareness, lust, greed, ego and apathy. Any one of these will cause an individual to destroy themselves. You must overcome these tendencies in order to have us contact you directly. Purify yourself and the wisdom you will earn will be gratifying to you and us for we have come to a point where we have to consider the limitations of the minds, the receptiveness, the average intelligence of those of your plane of existence.

We are all part of Christ. We are not individual entities outside of Christ. We are all individuals within Christ. That is why you are all brothers and sisters, for you are all part of the same whole. You are all individual expressions of the same Christ Spirit and you have within your being, millions and millions of cells which renew themselves daily as your spiritual being dictates. The whole, as you see it, is also the equivalent of a cell to the Christ Spirit. That is why each individual must meditate and find their particular avenue of expression so that the harmonics of their particular area of expression may be proper in the eyes of the Christ Spirit. When the individual has found their avenue of expression, they will be rewarded beyond their ability to comprehend.

You must understand that daily you give birth to new life; to new cells. There are cells which you give birth to the same as you give birth to whole bodies of cells in pregnancy. They will nurture themselves and will respond to the harmonics of your system. If there is any discordant avenue in your spiritual being it will reflect in precise order in your physical. You can renew any area of your physical in proportion to your thought intensity. If you think in error, erroneous cells will develop. Therefore, I am telling you and everyone that you have absolute control over the physical manifestation of your being. There are no external forces which could distort your being unless you allow this force to penetrate your thought power.

It has been known through expressions, that there are such things as poisonous verbiage or poisonous thought which will affect the well being of an individual if they accept these as being fact. For it is the acceptance of thought patterns which determines whether an outside force can modify, distort or re-arrange conditions within your harmonics. All the chemical elements are available to your physical for proper utilization in building a dynamic, vital, spiritual being. It is your responsibility to select the proper food elements required at the moment to build healthy tissue.

Do not be dismayed and do not tell yourself that you are incapable of overcoming for that is merely lack of faith.

Chapter 25

A New Civilization

IT IS A fact, as we have mentioned before, that there was upon this planet you call Earth, a civilization which was far advanced beyond your present state of being but by their own devices they devoured themselves. I pleaded with them to see the light but they were overcome by greed and destroyed everything around and about them. They built the Pyramids. They could travel at will and they did not need vehicles as you require them. Man today still has not attained the intelligence to do likewise. You will eventually excavate the remains of some of our temples at the head of the Nile. They laid waste the Nile Valley; they laid waste what you call Palestine; they laid waste the fertile valleys right through to China. Apathy for those around and about them is the basis for their destruction. There were but a few who survived and this again became the birth of a new civilization.

Here again this new civilization grew spiritually and once again was overcome by pride, greed and apathy and once again a certain few survived and once again civilization started to grow.

We are determined that this time we will not need to use a device such as a plague to thin out those who are undesirable. There is a renaissance as of the moment; a rekindling of the forces which were the basis of life. Those who do not believe and do not live according to the law will destroy themselves according to the law. Spirit will prevail. The struggle for the balance of power between the two forces no longer is at an equilibrium. The positive forces will prevail and multiply.

There are as many spheres of influences as there are stars in the sky. Each star has it's earth; each star has it's other planets. Each star has it's spiritual force which is inherently it's own. The universe is made up of many such influences which co-operate one with the other to make up the grand universe. So, your Christ Spirit, which is the spirit of your universe or your collection of planets, is inherently your total expression. Every other star has a similar arrangement around it. Now, if the intelligence of this so-called Christ Spirit amazes you, consider the intelligence of the Great I Am who is the accumulation of masses of such forces. That is why there is nothing impossible if one would tap this great force. But the individual must excite this force; the individual must attract this force; the individual must tickle the imagination of the potential of the desire to cause there various elements to co-operate and pool their resources to an end.

All is vibration. Each part of the universe and each universe has it's own set of harmonics. This is what causes the regularity in the systems to function as they do. You can tell by the manner of music, which the average entity digests, what will be the status of your universe. Contrary to the theories of the evolvement of species; of expressions of life, there has been refinement within the species. This is a very controversial subject in your universe. Your universe was conceived in thought; was planned in thought and was executed in vibration. Each component part was carefully placed relative to others. At the moment of beginning, every phase of life as you know it today was conceived simultaneously. There were times when they become disproportionate but then again the harmonics were caused to adjust themselves to return all to normalcy.

In the past decade, man has destroyed his balance but we are now in the process of changing this condition. It is only when the individual overcomes awareness of themselves as an independent being that your civilization will prosper and thrive. I cannot emphasize this strongly enough, for this was the downfall of many civilizations. You must overcome the tendency to use this great love force to control the destinies of those around and about you. Every entity is allowed by their own volition to attain the level and the harmonious relative position where they were placed in your environment without concern as to their importance relative to others. This is the key; this is the key that all are seeking but many are seeking importance alone not relative importance, but importance alone. This is a grave error.

We did not place every entity on this plane of existence to perform identical functions. You are part of a whole spirit force. You as an individual are an essential member. We therefore, place in your midst, various component parts in hopes that there will be a harmonious relationship each contributing it's essential vibration or harmonics for the benefit of all. When we see, by observation, that certain individuals are not harmonizing and refuse to harmonize, we find various means of plucking them from your midst and we place them elsewhere. Each individual life is a note; each group is as a bar in the great symphony of life.

Be not alarmed. There will be a great movement of the earth's crust in the very near future. You will feel the tremors physically. The effect on this system; the solar system, caused by a large meteor, will signal the beginnings of the revelation. There will be a bright, extremely bright halo, which will be visible in that day. It will circle your earth planet thrice and then return to the orbit around Mars. What it will be is a giant mass of electronic elements which make up the protective shield surrounding the planet Mars. It must be dramatic; spectacular, to have significance and it will be so. Shortly after this sign in the heavens you will receive all the necessary instruction on how to proceed to tap directly this powerful source of energy.

There will be a tremendous man-made explosion purely by accident in the Soviet sphere of influence. Then there will be a re-alignment in their political divisions and they will know that it is spiritually directed as a means of expression, for we are ever mindful of the contents of the wisdom which will be recorded through the instrument in your presence. (Here they are speaking of Rev. Robert Wagner, the medium through which this information was received.)

There will be multitudes which will, according to your experience, suddenly pass away. Those who remain will have learned the futility of material living. This is normal but medical science will be baffled. You will have many theories but no explanations.

The explanation is quite simple. There are those who will be chosen and those who do not qualify and they will be eliminated. The precise device used to eliminate them is immaterial. The fact of the matter is they must be eliminated. They will dissolve and be dissipated. There is no death as we know it. You only die when you lose your individuality. He who destroys the flesh does not destroy. There is only he who destroys the spirit. There is no destruction; there is merely a dispersal. This energy will be used to create the powerful source of communicative material for the benefit of those who remain. You will all witness baptism, for it was not until Jesus of Nazareth was baptized by the light that He preached the truth. He gave you the law. You will then individually receive instructions as to how you must proceed. Prepare yourself. There will be a complete re-birth of emotional manifestation amongst man. You have coined the word 'love'. You will see those around and about you in a new light. You will have overcome suspicion and mistrust. You will have overcome all phases of egotism.

This information, we feel, is essential for it will take a period of time to prepare yourselves for there will be a wave of energy, call it electronic force; call it cosmic force; call it what you will, passing into your influence. Those who are prepared will survive and those who are not prepared will disappear, dissipate or pass on normally. They will not all pass on dramatically in an instant but will pass on proportionately to their lack of faith over a period of a year and a half. The undesirable elements will have dissipated themselves from your influence. From the moment of this great wave on there will be no more conflict amongst man.

Chapter 26

Out of The Darkness Into The Light

WE DO NOT speak unless there is an attitude which is proper. This is a serious situation. This is not a condition other than deep communication. It is extremely important that you cleanse your minds of frivolous thoughts so that your vibrations can become pure and fine enough for us to guide our harmonics to you.

A great number of you are not convinced in your souls of your spiritual aspect of life. Many still approach life from a materialistic point of view. Now, you desire the peace, the harmonics and the uplifted feeling one receives from spiritual existence but you cling to your material approach and then you wonder why we do not contact you directly. Many still approach our presence with limitations they place on themselves. It is with great effort that we adjust our vibration to contact you. It should be a similar effort on your part to cleanse your hearts and minds of curiosity and material thoughts. You profess that you are spirit and that which you feel and observe around and about you is a reflection or a manifestation of spirituality or spirit thought. You claim to believe that reality is spirit but you do not practice this. When you have learned to overcome the so-called reality of the senses, you too will be able to contact the higher realm and converse with the higher realm without the aid of the Master. You must believe as He believed and you will have that which you seek, The only reason for the delay is materialistic limitations you have placed upon yourselves. Once you firmly believe in you hearts that you are spirit; that your physical is merely a reflection or manifestation of your spirit and once you contact us in spirit; once you set your material thoughts and your material approach aside and contact us in spirit; you will have opened an avenue of expression of communication that is limitless.

In the process of thinking spiritually you overcome fear for there is no fear in spiritual thinking. There is no anxiety in spiritual thinking. Yes, there is awareness and alertness. Most people are not aware of what is happening around and about them because they are so concerned with their individual entity that they cannot see or sense these conditions around and about them. This is the greatest stumbling block of man. You seek spiritual food but from a material point of view. We will feed you and we will satisfy your hunger but you must worship the Father in Spirit, for the Father is Spirit. We are all part of the Father. I am part of the Father and I have been chosen, so you have been chosen also. I have overcome the limitations of material thought as you must overcome the limitations of material thought. You can do it if you so desire.

God gave Moses twenty one tablets instead of ten but He destroyed them for He felt that mankind was so engrossed in lust that it was felt that man would ignore the information and distort it. So we denied man this information. As Jesus of Nazareth said as He sat by the well. 'you drink of these waters, I drink of the food of the waters from above.' That is how He fed the multitudes. He fed them spiritually. They all went into deep trance and were fed spiritually. I know you wonder about this for you cannot understand how a few fishes and loaves of bread could have fed the multitudes but they were overwhelmed with spiritual thought and knowing the reality of thought, there were sufficient people in their group who were touched so deeply that their thoughts became material reality and the loaves and fishes were created by their thoughts. This is as it was.

This is one of the laws, that you can think positively enough, firmly enough, pure enough to create that which you would have. Spiritual beings know no frustration for there are no limits to that which you can accomplish if you live according to spirit law. You place limits upon yourselves so that you do not have to put forth the effort to accomplish what you profess you wish to accomplish. It takes effort and purity of thought to overcome material limitations. Do not waste your time with materialistic approaches to your temple. I must impress upon you the relative importance of approach. You must meditate to prepare yourself in anticipation and be receptive. Ask that you be placed in a proper position relative to the whole and be satisfied to be part of a great force. Each of you is essential. We cannot expand our influence unless we have those through which we can express ourselves. You have been chosen as others have been chosen and you are capable of the higher realm if you would.

To us this is a sacred moment. We wish that you would treat it as such. You want fantastic manifestations without the effort on your part but this cannot be. If you wish great manifestations you must believe, not hope, not wonder but believe. Know in you heart that these things are true and real. Seek and you shall find and as you dissipate your mental reservations one by one you will receive in great proportion until you have overcome all limitations.

I would like to talk to you concerning color. You know color is vibration. Every color has it's vibration range. White and black are two different vibration ranges. You look at the sun and you say the sun is white but the sun is all colors. If you mixed all the primary colors in exact proportion you will either end up with black or white, If mixed properly, they will be white. Your sun is the source of all light on your planet and all the surrounding planets of the sun. The sun is alive; the sun is pure thought; the sun is pure vibration and as one gains spiritual attitude, their vibration becomes brighter and whiter. Ultimately they become parts of the sun. There is no such thing as lost energy. That which is emitted from the sun returns to the sun for there is eternity. Vibration and thought are indestructible. As you vibrate, every thought is a series of parallel vibrations and every vibration has it's own color and as your thoughts change so does the color harmonics change. Every thought pattern has it's own color combination. We observe these color combinations and we read the thoughts. This is the deice we use to identify individuals on the earth plane. The purer your thoughts the more intense the light and the more readily we can identify you. We seek out avenues of expression in this way.

I cannot give you a precise definition for each color for there are as many shades and tones of vibration as there are cells in your body buy there are basic categories in which certain vibrations lie which may be useful to you once your vibration has risen to a level where you can see what you call aura. There are times when you see the aura as you would the Northern Lights radiating from the individual. This is normal for as your thoughts change from one subject to another or one thought to another so does you thought vibration change and the color combinations change and the intensity of the various colors changes with every thought.

Do not fear black. This may surprise you but black is the foundation upon which we build. Those of you who see black please do not be fearful of failure for as you develop in this work, the deeper the black will become for then and only then have you displaced all material thought from your countenance. Then you look into this blackness with anticipation and you will see coming out of this blackness, the thought pattern which will take the shape of an object or an individual and as you anticipate and accept, you will see this condition manifest clearer and clearer until it becomes real in your mind. You will remember the remark, 'out of the darkness came light' and it will always be so. Out of the purity of the black will come the light. This is contrary to your accepted thoughts but first you must create the black; the purity of thought, before we can give you the light. So anticipate cleansing your thought patterns and creating the blackness and then anticipate knowing that every thought has a combination of colors. Contrary to what many people have been telling you., there is no definition for each individual color.

When you wish to communicate, first you dismiss any and all thought from your mind. You create blackness. Then for an instant, concentrate your thought without reservation into the either, as you call it, and you will suddenly create an intense concentration of light which we see readily. We immediately adjust our vibration to this light and cause the proper force to attach itself to this light to fulfill the need of the one who intended to place the desire for food and service.

We show vitality in the greens basically. The yellows are generally desire thoughts of service to another of a higher nature. Your reds and oranges are basically the drive force or activity thoughts. Your blues are peace and relaxation. So, therefore, when you have a combination of red and blue and you cause lavender, violet or purple depending upon the intensity of thought, you have a color combination that places you in a spiritual identity and the deeper the purple the more spiritual minded you are. I hope this explains your colors for this is the information I believe you should have as of the moment.

Chapter 27

Living Within The Law

EACH OF YOU is placed upon your planet to attain a means of refinement of your beings. When each individual is working toward that which he was placed here for, he finds himself in a state of being of complete harmony with his surroundings and his means of compensation will be more than adequate for his needs. We do not see all of those who are working, for many become lost or lose their enthusiasm. We make an effort to cause these individuals to find themselves but if they do not do so, we abandon them for future dissolvableness into the whole.

Sin is ignorance of the law. The devil is synonymous with sin. The state of heaven is synonymous with harmonious existence. You do not necessarily have to be on a higher plane to be in the harmonious state of being. It is easier to become harmonious on a higher plane for you have overcome most of your ignorance of the law.

Man speaks of birth control and this amuses us to no end, for man has no control over birth. We will not allow more entities than are required for the harmony of the whole mass. We do not have energy to dispose of indiscriminately. We are quite conscious of energy and it's developments. This group which seems to be favoring this birth control technique are a group of intellectuals and their whole avenue of expression, when you analyze it, is to cause them to be judges of right from wrong, good from evil and to eliminate the great mass of what you call the common man so that the world will be full of intellectuals, such as they are. I know they use the excuse of food production as a basic argument. We have no reason to place more people on your planet than are essential to the well being of the Christ Spirit, for you are all essential parts of the Christ Spirit. The reason we have so-called excess beings, is that on many occasions you are in a transitional stage of development and you have the residue of the previous condition of existence and the beginnings of the next stage of existence intermingling one with the other and this is the state of your planet today.

Within a period of from ten to fifteen years, this transition from the materialistic approach of existence will have replaced itself with the spiritual approach of acceptance. There, of necessity, has to be friction and there is normally friction between the spiritual approach and the material approach. We are constantly, as I said before, refining the individual souls, constantly purifying sin from their being. They must experience events in their life so that they may cause themselves to release certain inharmonious thought patterns in their beings. Your purpose is to contribute your share within the limits established by the law for the benefit of all facets of the Christ Spirit. Know this and know it well for the Christ Spirit will prevail.

Look within yourself; ask yourself, 'what must I do with that which was allotted to me, so that I may be a true vehicle though which this great intelligence may flow?' Since this great law is a gift just as your existence is a gift, you must learn to transmit this law to the others around and about you who are essentially establishing a phase of the great law. Man can fool with this just so long but he does not have the control that he envisions.

We mentioned music before. Do not discount music, for music is the food of the soul. Faith, when underscored, is the knowledge of a supreme being. The Great I Am is not an individual sitting on a throne. The Great I Am has many heads. One head for each facet of existence but all part of one great body. All the avenues of expression around and about you, each in their own right, has it's own supreme power; supreme thought pattern that regulates it's very existence from the higher realm. This may help you to understand the total concept. When you have faith in your Master Teacher and have established a proper, humble approach to your essential part in the overall symphony, you will find that you will lead a rewarding existence. When you place yourself into the guidance of your Master, he will make available to you at all times, powers required to fulfill your portion of the great whole. All powers are available to all souls in greater or lesser degrees depending on their mission. Here we place equal importance in all missions.

Even though I am part of the great fountainhead of the great intelligence, I know that I am powerless without my avenues of expression all the way down the ladder. You are part of me, I am part of you. We need each other. Ultimately, you will find that you sacrifice nothing of your liberty by living within the law and opening your avenues of contact; that you will not only find yourself with greater feelings of belonging but greater deeds of fulfillment will be expressed through your individuality. You will have expanded your avenues of expression, for as it says in the 'Book', the truth shall make you free. You will suddenly have dropped all restriction on your movements within your sphere of influence. By humbling yourself and placing yourself in a position of being perfect vehicles of expression you will find the tremendous expansion of your ability to express yourself. I am not speaking of controlled servitude but avenues of expression. These are the rewards of which we speak.

There is another fallacy which says that we will pluck from your midst an individual entity. This is only done in severe instances. Normally, the individual creates the situation within their erroneous approach to the reality of life which causes them to dissolve themselves. You must fear only the fact that you may create a situation of which I just spoke. So do not use this crutch in your rationalization. The force that caused you to be established on this plane of existence watches over you as a parent to a child, generally guiding you and advising you throughout your existence. They attempt to restore to reality those who will fulfill the mission. For the mission is more important than any individual.

All matter is harmonious and when you disturb the harmony in general you create a condition of sin and this is a misplaced energy pattern. It tends to try to grow within itself it justify itself. It tries to validate itself on an individual basis. That is what you call the devil. We shed tears up here when we see entities who have such a potential create conditions which make their existence untenable. We have compassion; more compassion than you are capable of on your plane, for we are not so foolish as to allow one or two in proportion, to destroy the general plan of the general harmonics of each phase of life. When you have released sin from your countenance, which is fear, doubt and indulgence, you will have famous power as demonstrated by Jesus. One in whom we are well pleased.

Chapter 28

Rebirth

Now MY FIRST point I'm sure may shock many people. When one analyzes life from the spiritual point of view, not a material point of view, your attitudes are almost diametrically opposed.

Considering what you call birth control—since there is no death can there be birth as such or is birth only a simple re-entry into a physical temple? Since what can kill the flesh cannot kill the spirit. There is no death. Since there is no death there is no birth. What I am saying in essence, is that a spirit entity chooses a material body or temple, we prefer to call it and if this spirit entity, by some means or other, is denied the use of this temple, you have not killed the spirit entity, you have only destroyed a material temple. And likewise, since spirit is eternal, except for the disposition of the God Power, while it can be dissipated, as you have been given information on in previous lessons, only the God Power can dissipate a spirit entity and cause it to decease as an entity, but it's material and vibratory elements are dispersed amongst others for further use in life.

There is no loss of life in the spirit world. There may be dispersal but never a loss. Those who do not attain a level ultimately are dispersed. Those who attain a level retain their identity and continually work for the betterment of themselves and their fellowman. So we place very little importance on what happens to the material temple for the spirit being. If denied the material temple, one can choose another and develop this as they see fit. So, when they speak of birth control methods, we do not frown for we eventually do control the temple of expression.

If one conception is denied us, we do not become alarmed but we seek out another. It is that simple. And by the same token, if a spirit being finds their material temple not serving them as they know it should, if they had, through foolish acts, foolish thought patterns, created a condition which they feel is non-returnable to harmony and they choose to destroy this temple so that they can seek out a new beginning for expression we see no objection in this. We know that these two elements or patterns of thought are contrary to material man's thinking but from a spiritual point of view, if one has a garment which does not please them do they throw it away, give it away or dispose of it in some other manner and purchase a new garment? I know this will cause eyebrows to raise but when you consider that only that which matters is spiritual; when you consider all life is a convenience to your spirit not spirit a convenience of your body you will understand.

In the Orient, they had honorable means of destroying a physical being. That is, it placed itself in a position for continuing along a certain pattern and if this pattern has become untenable, it is considered honorable to destroy this being. One must examine one's motives deeply in destroying one's temple. It is admitting failure. This we understand. Thought patterns which created this condition can be reversed. If one would get themselves to the point of analyzing themselves and being truthful with themselves they would find a basis or motivation for regeneration for their soul being and this temple which they have so sorely abused is not to blame for their failures. It is merely a reflection of their misuse of the spiritual being.

It is good for a person who is away from the reality of spiritual thinking to be put in the position to face the facts of their failures and then analyze the points and from this point on they could become a very strong spiritual being. There are many in your existence who at this point of decision, grew strong and then failed; vibrant people subsequent to their day of so-called tragedy. Very often from tragedy, there is an effective spiritual re-birth in the individual. We do not condemn destroying one's temple, but we do frown for we do reward greatly those who have gotten to the point where they finally and firmly are aware of themselves and build a firm foundation on a moment of despair.

We are speaking of re-birth spiritually as of this moment. When we speak of re-birth spiritually, we are not talking about material re-birth. Spiritual re-birth can be attained at any state of existence. There is no physical involvement in re-birth. Since there is no death we would wish you not to mourn at setting aside of the spiritual temple for when the spirit has left that temple, it becomes inert. As long as the spirit is in the temple it is vital. When the spirit leaves the temple or body it is as nothing; only ash. It goes from whence it came.

We do not believe in mourning. At times we would rejoice at the individual spirit being released from the limitations of the material temple which they created. We rejoice that they have an opportunity now to examine themselves. There are times when a spirit entity passes over, as you say, that go into a state of being which you would call sleep-rest. This rest may last for hours, days, years, hundreds of years depending upon the individual. Then you go into a state of being where they become oriented and we pluck from this great mass of entities who are in deep sleep, those who will be useful to the overall spirit program. We send them into oriented classes and when they have been oriented in the direction we know they are capable of developing, we send them down to seek out a temple which they can use to perform their mission. This may explain why progression of mankind is not by accident. There is this vast reserve which we have available at all times. So, when one passes on, they always go through these two stages if they are spiritually oriented. Some never leave this pool. Others visit this pool for only brief moments, depending on our needs for the benefit of mankind.

It is possible and it is probable that an entity could be deceased, as you call it, in one temple and we would reprocess that entity in a matter of days and have that entity re-enter another temple in a matter of days or hours. This we do quite often. There are times when we know there is a time element when a certain thought pattern is important to the welfare of man and we will not seek out a child but we will seek out what you call a mature temple and place this entity into this temple and will jointly use this temple with another being and ultimately will dispose of the being that is in that temple and bring that being back to the pool. This we have done. That is a case of so-called life and death which you are unaware of but it is a reality in our eyes. The transition is never that great in personality but someone who has learned the desire of attainment. This may sound inhuman but we are not human. We are spirit and our mission is more important than the temple or the vehicle which must accomplish it.

You think nothing of destroying a building and building a new edifice in its place. We are no different. Your temples, your bodies, as you call them, are temples or buildings to us. You speak of tearing a building down because of progress. There is a similarity; a different means, different vehicles, but similar.

Speaking about marriage—this is another tradition which we have definite opinions about. We believe that as long as two spirit entities are in harmony and are working jointly and collectively on their missions there is a marriage, as you call it. The litigation is spiritual not physical. So therefore, the statement that was made through Jesus of Nazareth and other prophets is correct; that if a marriage is built on harmony and mutuality of purpose no man can cast it asunder; no physical being can destroy this unity. Any marriage that is built on physical attraction and not mutuality of purpose in being while sanctioned by man made law or not is not a marriage in our eyes and is doomed to failure. Though a marriage which is constituted in heaven, as you call it, is a marriage of mutuality. We well sanctify such a joining and the joining will become beautiful in relationship. In our eyes there is marriage as long as there is harmony. This is as we see it. I know man must have his laws for material lineage; for material transferal of worldly goods but we do not consider material lineage whatsoever. There may be three or four issues of a material existence and we would choose to put three or four diverse entities into that atmosphere. The choice is ours.

It is true that parents have a certain amount of influence on the spiritual growth of a child but ultimately the child emerges as an individual entity when the material temple has matured. Parents may have control over the ultimate growth of the entity but their influence would be minimal if the spirit being is strong. If the spirit being is weak initially, parental influence may be as much as 50% to 60%. That is why parents and children both become bewildering to each other at a point in their relationship on maternal expression. You call it the generation gap. There is a great generation gap caused very simply by the average entity today being higher spiritually than the parent who allegedly conceived them. We are introducing a whole new stream; a whole new flow or as we call it, a renaissance of spiritual attainment of a worldwide plane for the beings have become overly materialistic in their attitudes and we decided rather than try to evolve these entities we decided to let them destroy themselves spiritually speaking. Eventually they will materially send a new influx of spirituality on your plane of existence. That is the reason for the generation gap. It is your only salvation.

Search your motives; search your values and be re-born. It is not to late. Analyze yourself with indifference and emotional lack. Analyze yourself; analyze your values, your position and then change the thought patterns as required and be re-born spiritually.

When the Bible spoke of death; as the days of death of sinners—those days are at hand. The sinners will die; the spiritual will live. There will be a great social upheaval because of the re-birth of man's concern for man not man's concern for position in society. There is a tremendous difference in our eyes. One must be concerned for man not of position. One must be concerned for the welfare of the movement of mankind, not for self attainment. For he who gives of himself in line of his mission will attract to himself all those who proceeded him who have attained this level and man will glorify this one for his works. He will be superior in the eyes of his fellowman.

Chapter 29

Summary

WE WISH TO maintain the individual desire for inner peace for this is the basis of all understanding. The individual must overcome awareness of self. The individual must be completely engrossed in that which is around and about him to make proper adjustments in his own sphere for each individual is a god-power component. Each individual, as you see them, is a center core around which many vibratory influences revolve. You are like the nucleus of an atom. You have around and about you, individually, influences which are attracted to you which revolve around and about you and intermingle with your soul personality the same as the universe has a sun and many planets around and about it. You are the sun and you attract to you the individual influences which augment your personality and as you arise or as you ascend to higher planes of existence, you merely purify your individual soul and you drop the influences of the lower plane and attract to you influences from the higher plane. The combined effort of these influences and your purified soul causes you to ascend and ascend and ascend.

The sun, as you see it, is a high concentration of soul power. It is the same light you see when you are blessed and baptized only the sun is a mass of such lights; a highly concentrated mass of such lights and this is the source of all light and life. The solar energy is spiritual in nature. Man can record this spirit force but does not know the cause. Man likes to give accord to electricity but does not know the source.

Remember, you as individuals are growing universes within yourselves only on a minor scale. That is why some of you can contact us more readily than others and when you realize this fact you realize first and foremost that you have the control of the spirit influences that you attract to you. They do not come in enforcedly and replace others. You are constantly surrounded by influences from the higher realm looking for an avenue of expression and they are constantly seeking ways and means of communication but they have to wait patiently for the individuals at your plane of existence to ascend to the level which will allow them to communicate. Your desire is a motivating force. Your desire to serve is quite important. In order to have ascension your desire to serve must become greater than awareness of self or self indulgence. Then once you have clarified your role and humbled yourself to your mission though faith and the Father's love, you will ascend. You must not just merely wish for something to happen but you must firmly desire this path. Overcome all doubts. Overcome ALL doubts. For doubt is the enemy of your progress.

We carefully examine the motive. In my sessions I have spoken of many technicalities, origins of life, food for life but motive is the basis of action; motive is the basis of movement; motive is the guiding force for without proper motive there is no positive action. The great teachers had great motives and patience. They were persistent and had faith. Faith is merely the knowledge that all things are possible if one has the proper motive. Motive is the key. Proper motive is the 'action trigger'. We are all part of the God Power. We, as a unit, can accomplish that which is necessary at any given moment and when one's light is strong enough to attract our attention, we immediately assimilate this thought motive and if we feel that it is worthy, we call in the forces to accomplish the end.

All knowledge is worthless without motivating force. This is my key. This is my admonishment. Examine your motive before you desire action. Increase your faith before you implement action because purpose without faith has a weak motivation. You must be strong in faith and pure in motive to accomplish the great works which many of the Masters accomplished.

Power is not external. The power is from within. You must learn to rely on self. I am not saying pooling your resources is not desirable but the only means of making contact with your higher self and again with higher selves, is through internal recognition of your spiritual being as being without change or restrictions. Man creates the thoughts which limit the activities in his spiritual being. You must one by one remove the shackles created by the thoughts of those around and about you and give yourself complete freedom of action and thought which is your inherent heritage.

THE TRUTH SHALL MAKE YOU FREE. There is no earth bound spirit or earthy entity who can restrict your spiritual activity unless you allow it to be so. You, as an individual, can free yourself of all fear and anxiety and live in the positive anticipation of the moment fearless of the future. As Jesus of Nazareth said, "You can do as I do and greater things then I, can you do, if you believe as I believe."

Many of us spoke with Him; many of us worked through Him as the need arose. Develop His faith now with us and you too will be great in the eyes of many for to be great you must lose yourself. You must lose awareness of self and become an essential part of the over-all. This is the key. First a drop of water strikes the soil and it filters to an inlet; into a brook; into a stream; into a river and then into an ocean. Which is greater? The power of the ocean or the power of the drop of water? Consider this. Most are content to be the drop of water. Few see the wisdom of becoming part of the ocean. That is a fallacy of man. He is content with being a drop of water. Your horizons are endless.

I am sure that if you read these works over on many occasions that you would imprint in your minds the steps; the avenues required for re-birth in the light. Unless you are born again and re-think, readjust your thinking to the purity of that time of your so-called physical birth, you will not enter the higher realm; you will not be re-born in spirit; you will not receive the rewards of spiritual thinking. We are not asking you to deny your daily requirements of your body. All we ask of you is to take the proper relative attitude towards your body and your spirit. We are speaking of the relativity of spirit and your flesh. When you have placed each in it's proper position you will find that you have thrown the yokes of sin from your shoulders. When we speak of sin we speak of sin as being the devices of man created by man for the control of others. So when you are born in sin you are born in an atmosphere of man made devices for the control of man. This and this alone is sin. Crime is the result of sin.

The Christ Spirit is the controlling force of your sphere of influence. He, if you want to use this vernacular, is not a God but a great force. He is a symphony; a complete spiritual body. He is the motivating force behind all activity on your plane of existence. The reason we use the word body is to cause you to associate the complexity of this great force in a manner in which you can visualize. The Christ Spirit has no form. The Christ Spirit also has a greater force and there are greater forces than these again. You must be aware of the fact that the force; the great intelligence which controls the movements of great bodies as well as the movements of the finest of living mechanisms, must have intelligence greater than it, which is capable of perfecting a complete balance of elements of life.

Now these forces are available to all under proper conditions. When one has attained a level of intelligence capable of absorbing the harmonies at the higher vibratory rate they can accomplish great influential positions in your plane of existence. This repeats itself in other universes of which there are countless numbers staggering beyond your capability of comprehension. Each of these has an equivalent of your Christ Spirit. The Christ Spirit manifests basically through the one you call Melchizedek. Many referred to Melchizedek as the Father. Jesus of Nazareth spoke of him as the Father; the source closest to the ultimate.

Contrary to a common misconception by the average man and woman on your plane of existence, we will say there is death, but not in the manner in which you understand. We have already expounded on the theory of death. When we find an entity who is tending to disrupt the harmonics of the great force we dissipate this entity and use it as food for other embryos of thought. Once we have established a contact there is, what you feel to be, a clairvoyant. As long as the individual stays in their realm of influence that is compatible with his surroundings, he will progress. It is when the individual willfully digresses from his established pattern of harmonics that he becomes disillusioned, upset and restless and this restlessness transfers through to others and consequently causes disharmony in a group and it spreads throughout the others who are affected.

At times we have fostered conflicts. You may ask why? But we had to disrupt the complacency of the minds of the individuals to stimulate them to great concentrations of thought. Through these devices we have accelerated to a great extent, the general level of intelligence of man. When man has no goal, there is no movement. There must be a constant flow of energies, otherwise this great Christ force will tend to regress. Man's general intelligence has risen to a level whereby we do not require artificial stimuli to cause him to seek; to search for greater achievement. The need for devices of conflict are now no longer required for progress. The percentage of those whose intelligence has risen closer to the Christ Spirit is far greater now than it was a decade ago and infinitely greater than at the time of Jesus of Nazareth. You must remember a basic statement of this teacher of life who came to enlighten you in the ways of the brotherhood. He attained this level early in the recordings of manifestations and it is true that from time to time this force concentrated itself in what you call an individual being. As the intelligence in the universe increased you were given greater wisdom in understanding generally.

You must understand that many of these Holy Books which you call Holy we do not call Holy. They are recordings of the intelligence of that stage of existence of the world; the universe in which you live, had attained at the time. The writings which we have dictated to you at this moment are what you would call the "Holy Book Updated". This supersedes all others. This does not replace but it augments and brings up to date the information which we wish and feel is appropriate as of this time.

Concentrate on causing these recordings to be in a language properly understood by all your fellowmen. This material must be protected according to man's law upon the release for the benefit of all. You are part of the Great I Am. You have been chosen and you will continue and progress only when you overcome the awareness of self; only when you overcome the tendency of being concerned with your individual mission as being the center of all activity. When you become aware of the fact that you are individually, an essential factor and when you look around and about you and you discover that you are essential to the well being of all forces of a particular nature surrounding you, you will realize that you are all dependent or interdependent whichever way you wish to assimilate this information. You are part of a great, great body beyond your comprehension and when you realize that you as an individual being; an essential part of the whole, can activate the whole by proper concentration, the thought pattern transfers itself to the governing area and can trigger great activity; great concentration at any given moment. Your force in co-operation with those around and about you can accomplish these great ends. Each individual force or sphere has common vibrations. It is only when the individual tends to leave this area of influence that they become distressed or ill.

Illness is merely a state caused by the individual attempt to work beyond your harmonics which are not normal to you causing distress in your being. So, when one wishes to become perfectly at ease one must ask to overcome the individual eccentrics and become re-harmonized; become an essential harmonic force properly attuned to the whole. You call this Prayer. This is the opening of your being to the forces which can and will re-adjust your harmonics to a proper level.

Understand that prayer is not asking for something or thanking someone. It is for you to find yourself; find your part, your essential part of the eternal order of things; that it be shown to you and that you become a worthy essential member of the Great I Am.

Part II

Chapter 30

Basics of Physical Life

SOME ARE CONCERNED unduly as to the mineral content of normal water. Minerals in the water system are just as important to a healthy temple as spirit food. Don't be alarmed, for you must realize it is the same water; it is the same minerals, the same acids, the same alkali that your various plants selectively absorb to produce the food value for your physical temple.

If you drank water in its natural state; the same water that your plant life drinks, you would have received these minerals in their normal state and would benefit accordingly. The plants do, as I said earlier, use selective absorption. That is why certain fruits and vegetables contain different combinations of essential elements for your system. You call these vitamins.

Temperature; ambient temperature as well as internal temperature does have a chemical action on these combinations. This temperature causes a chemical reaction which causes heat. The heat generated by your body to warm your body, is caused by chemical reaction one to another. You have concentrates in your system which when they contact certain elements, mineral or otherwise, react accordingly as far as food ingestion is concerned. Each individual must, by experimentation or deep meditation, adjust his or her system to the needs of their system. Therefore, there are no set rules which cover the general scope of vital foods. We strongly advise that you eat your foods as near to the normal state as you possibly can.

There is a group who believes in fasting in an attempt to eliminate poison from their system and to give their system a rest. This is a fallacy. Your system thrives on activity. The sedentary person will age at a far greater rate then an active person. Nothing ages the physical body faster than inactivity. Since you are building millions of new cells daily, you need the proper combination to chemicals in your system daily. It is when you are not receiving a proper balance of chemicals, that you become ill. If you must eat flesh, here again, eat it in as close to its natural state as is practical. If you place this flesh in a high temperature condition you cause chemical reaction in the area affected by the high temperatures and you create indigestible compounds which may make you feel full and uncomfortable after eating such a meal. These rendered elements tend to clog your bladder, your kidneys, and various organs of minor character in your system and cut their efficiency and capacity to produce the proper chemicals for further expansion of the cell-body. So therefore, with these organs working at a capacity which is not normal, you find your blood system and your nervous system clogged with these elements, for the body has difficulty in disposing of them and becomes heavy because of an accumulation of this material in your system.

With careful diet you can eat the proper foods and drink the proper liquids which in turn will give you chemical balance in your system which will tend to reject these pollutants in your system. This is an attempt to cause you to understand the basics of physical life. It would be beneficial for you to drink pure spring water taken from a pristine area for one could live on water from a spring indefinitely.

Once we are purged of these toxins, as the doctors call them, or irritants to the system, the body becomes slender and normal and the aging process is slowed considerably. This cleaning of the vital system of the body or temple, is essential for the vitality required for spiritual attainment. Food, liquids, exercise to stimulate the flow of these liquids through your system are a necessary balance of your development. I must emphasize properly the fact that the food elements or chemical elements are of extreme importance to your system and your ability to ascend and to make proper contact with what you call the spiritual realm.

It is also essential that you go into your slumber in a meditative frame of mind. Any chemical that you introduce into your system which will create an imbalance, will cause a temporary excitement, the same type of excitement that you could see at the moment when a teakettle goes to a boil. Therefore, we strongly advise against sedentary supplements or high acid concentrates. Refrain from medicinal tablets unless their intake would supplement and not disturb. You need not eat an austere diet, for there are natural flavors within these foods you eat which are palatable to your system.

Now, your taste buds are not put there to enjoy the flavor of the food—that is not their prime function. Those taste buds are placed there to ascertain the nature of the chemical composition of the food you are placing in your mouth. Every organ in your body has a certain area in your mouth or certain number of taste buds located properly, which excite your various organs into activity. If you do not wish indigestion, you must eat slowly enough so that your taste buds can have contact with the food long enough to trigger the various enzymes and digestive juices for the benefit of your physical. This may sound oversimplified, but it is essential to your well being. This is basic and I cannot emphasize it firmly enough.

If you wish, what you call physical medium-ship, we must provide the proper foods oriented to the climate one finds themselves in. There is no such thing as a universal food because your environmental conditions vary. We change your food requirements with the season. Do not become emotionally involved while you are consuming nourishment, for each of your organs react to emotion. If one remains emotionally stable. the cause of the feared disease you call cancer can be reversed by proper food intake. It is caused by persistent, non-uniform intake. All the chemicals are available to you to effect a permanent reversal and when you place yourself in meditation, we can select the proper combinations in your being needed to benefit you.

The planetary vibrations affect your ability to digest various elements and utilize them for the benefit of the physical, for each one born under various planetary influences must vary their diet in proportion to the influence they are under at any given moment. As of now, we have not established at your plane of existence, the proper cycle for your requirements, but if each of you would meditate briefly on arising, we would inspire you as what to eat for that day which would be proper.

It may be of interest to you that the thistle, burdock, dandelion and milkweed all have high concentrations of ingredients which are of extreme food value for your physical. Therefore, everyone must be aware of the planetary positions in our diet for high spiritual attainment. Getting back to these so-called weeds which man has discarded from his diet, are found the most important sources of energy which will keep your organs in proper functioning order. It is true that they have a bitter taste, but we used this same bitter taste for healing purposes on several occasions. You can derive these chemicals from these weeds, put them in combination with other chemicals which are palatable and we call these elements spirit food—spirit growth food.

Chapter 31

Essentials to Good Health

YOUR FOOD INTAKE and proper emotional stability are the essentials to good health. Most of the people in this realm of life are suffering from malnutrition. There is a movement which is gaining crescendo throughout the world in which people now are becoming conscious of what they are to consume to live a normal existence. It is not unusual to create any illness you wish to desire as proof. By just deviating your eating habits, you can create most physical symptoms of improper eating.

The closer you can eat foods to their natural state, the healthier your body becomes. The average person overcooks their food. The normal roughage which is caused by foods in their natural state is eliminated by overcooking and consequently you have a milky mass going through your system with no bulk to cleanse the linings of your abdominal tracts. It is quite necessary for you to have roughage in your system to scrape gently and deep cleanse the little nodes that reach into your intestinal tract which absorb chemicals required by each organ as the digested food passes through the system.

Many peel an apple before they eat it but if you ate the apple skin and the apple seed and threw away the rest of it, you would derive great benefit. You peel the potato but it is the potato skin where the great nutritional value is. If you must eat corn, eat whole kernel corn, but eat it as nearly raw as you can. Now if you insist upon cooking your food, all your food is doing is giving you a volume or bulk and you have essentially destroyed the nutritional value. It is true that theoretically, you eat certain foods to derive certain benefits from them but this is only in their natural state. You may find that if you eat wax beans that are just washed, you will have a very chewable, delicious vegetable. If you have eaten raw peas you will know the difference in the taste is dramatic from the cooked version.

One of the greatest causes of indigestion is the fact that the average person cooks their food to such a soft state that they merely have it put it in their mouth and swallow it. Your saliva glands are placed there to give you a preliminary digestion of the food you put in your mouth, but the average person does not chew sufficiently long to create the saliva sufficient to digest their food and they have a heaviness in their stomach. They say the food was wrong and they are correct; it was too soft.

You are recommending what you call dietary supplements. This is not wrong, for when we experimented we discovered that one could live on vitamins exclusively in conjunction with a fruit type liquid. We experimented with this for a three months period whereby the first two meals of the day were vitamin concentrated as dictated by us and the third meal was a normal so-called meal and we discovered that the abundance of energy was tremendous. The physical consumes food to ingest the proper minerals, salts and acids. Most of your vitamins are acids to sustain your physical being. Each organ of your body requires different quantities and different mixtures of vitamins and minerals. It is through your intestinal tract that these various organs are fed, so if these food elements are in your system they are readily absorbed by these cilia which extend into your tract and the organ functions normally.

Now, if you eat improperly, your body retains this liquid mess hopefully to receive the proper nutrition it requires and consequently you build up a reserve of unusable fat in your system only because you have not received the proper nourishment. This is the cause of coronary conditions. This is the cause of ulcerous conditions. Your organs are functioning in an imbalanced relationship. If your organs are all fed their normal requirements, the system will balance within itself and there will be an impossibility for what you call thrombosis, ulcers, arthritic conditions and I could name many, many other conditions.

There is no such thing as taking a vitamin concentrate for a specific condition. You must take your vitamins in combination, for as you strengthen one area, you do not wish to put a strain on another area. So we take all vitamins and all minerals constantly. You may very your formulation from time to time for therapeutic reasons but you must take all vitamins and minerals all the time. This is very important. To repeat, you merely increase or decrease formulas temporarily to build up or strengthen or to re-balance your intake. When you have proper intake you do not feel bloated;

you do not have a throbbing headache; you do not have dull pains in your chest; you do not have a heavy feeling in your abdominal area and you have no difficulty in elimination. This is essential, for when one learns to eat properly, one must learn to relax properly for with every emotion there is a corresponding action from the glandular system in one's body. So it behooves the individual to remain calm and self-assured at all times.

Most people eat far more flesh than their body requires. If you would but concentrate on your roots, nuts, fruits and grains and eat flesh occasionally, you would find your well being enhanced. Chew your food well for this is extremely important. Honey is also an excellent food.

Rest, not necessarily sleep, is essential to one's well being. The theory of sleep is to dismiss all stresses of the day and you allow your body to relax to repair the damage which the day's emotional activities have created with the individual. If one could relax completely at intervals throughout the day, one would not require a long period of sleep. This sleep tradition is a man made law. This eating three meals a day is a man made law. Man has not learned to watch the infant. We insist that the infant eat when he is not hungry only because we decide he should eat. But we are slaves to tradition in that we must all eat at certain hours because that is customary.

There will be a strong renaissance of proper eating and resting habits. You see, you have complete control over this system or what you call the body. Don't concern yourself with the eating habits of others. It is not how much you eat, but how well you eat. One of the most common illnesses is caused by lack of vitamin B concentrate. There are times when it is necessary to increase your vitamin C, or D, or E, but by all means never neglect your unsaturated oils. These are extremely valuable in the functioning of your glands. Now, I am assuming that these supplements are in their natural state. If you grew your own fruits and vegetables under natural conditions and ate them under natural conditions, you would not require supplements.

Concerning exercises, the reason you age is because you become more sedentary in your nature. You need exercise to squeeze your blood vessels; to keep them healthy and you need exercise to cause this fluid to churn through the system to transfer these food elements along with oxygen to the various cells. You put on weight only because you do not have proper exercise. You allow cancerous conditions to create themselves for lack of exercise, for cancer is nothing more then a growth caused by the body's normal function of eliminating foreign elements within its structure. Whether these foreign elements are toxins which are allowed to develop in pockets and low circulation areas or whether a foreign element is introduced into the system is immaterial. It is the body's defensive structure which gets out of hand caused by emotion or improper eating. Whether in combination or individually, they can both induce and consume.

If you wish to prolong your physical life and live a healthy existence, this you must also remember; that in addition to your fluid system which you call blood, there is a second fluid system which you call your nervous system and this must be fed also. This fluid is basically derived from your unsaturated fats. We do not wish to see you get involved in strenuous exercise; we only wish that you find some means of exciting your nervous system.

If you take strenuous deep breathing exercises at each mealtime; if you would strain one muscle against the other prior to eating your meal, you would find that this generally is sufficient for longevity. Then obtain exercise through walking and moving about and you will find that with this formula you will extend your life span on the average of twenty five to thirty years actively with a minimum of harmonious action.

Weight lifting is good exercise but is considered strenuous if it strains beyond the normal capacity of the muscles. For then you are tearing down cells abnormally and they have to be replaced in an abnormal base. The moment you have to strain, you are destroying some cells that normally rest.

Chapter 32

A balanced Diet?

Now is the time for us to consider medication in it's true light. Medical Science is delving in great lengths with various chemicals to create various moods within the physical. Each individual normally creates these same chemical combinations from the elements they have received from their intake of food and liquids. The mood, at the time, determines which combination of chemicals are poured into the system. Every chemical necessary to proper health, is normally in the body, if one eats their meals according to God's Law. It is merely deficiencies of proper intake of chemicals which causes life to be sub-par. It is not intended that the body contain excessive amounts of any chemical. The chemical combinations which cause any disease are in every one's body, so likewise, the chemicals are within the being to cure every malfunction of the body. Illness is caused by imbalance of the necessary food intake in the system or emotional imbalance. These are the only two causes of physical symptoms of illness.

When one eats properly and when one lives in a relaxed atmosphere, illness cannot alter the perfect being. Every emotion triggers once again, various chemical elements and your physical reacts accordingly. That is why it is important to your well being that you consume the proper elements and to remain calm, cool and collected in your daily attitudes. It is true that one could consume excessive amounts of various nutritional elements in the system. Mankind, instinctively, is seeking a balanced diet depending on the nature of the individual as to whether a balanced diet would suit his condition better than the same balanced diet would suit another individual. Each diet must be framed around the personality aspects of the individual, for as one becomes habitually, emotionally oriented in a certain direction they consume an imbalance of chemicals. Consequently one must replenish these chemicals and this imbalance to maintain proper health.

There is no such thing as a balanced diet at all. This is a fallacy. In fact, as the personality of the individual changes, so must the diet or the intake change. Therefore, it is important that you have strong urges to consume or drink certain chemical elements and you must heed these thoughts, for your body will dictate to you the elements which it is lacking. Heed these thoughts. Do not question them. It is not necessary that you eat the same so-called balanced meal every time because your emotional strains vary from hour to hour and day to day. Therefore, your food intake must vary with this. You see, I am drawing a parallel or interdependence of emotion and actual consumption of food elements for proper health.

It is possible to consume too much of any one of these supplementary elements you call vitamins. It is better for you to consume all the elements on a daily basis, for all the elements are required for rebuilding cells essential to your body. As you know, many thousands of cells are created and abandoned every minute and if you have the proper chemical elements in your system you will grow normally. You must, and I cannot emphasize this strongly enough, consume all elements every day. You will have the urge to increase, add, or decrease various items, but this is all.

There are questions of weight control. When one's physical has all the proper elements with normal liquid introduced into the system, one's body throws off the toxins which are caused by your emotional disturbances and you body will become pliable and vital. No one who is consuming the proper elements and who is relaxed in their attitude could possibly become overweight, for it is lack of proper elements in your diet which causes your body to store up these elements in the system in hopes that the conditions, the elements required can be segregated from the so-called food consumed. Since the body is seeking out the missing elements it stores, you have to provide the right chemicals for it to find.

Consume the elements derived from natural grain. Eat fruits such as figs, dates, apricots and raisins. You should eat a small quantity of these daily, not all inclusive but one or the other. You must eat fruits of the basic variety such as apples, oranges, peaches and pears daily. The average person who tends to control their weight, eats too much in the line of salads. as you call them. It is true, for normal diet there must be a certain amount of grass in your system, for this is where you derive the chemicals you normally find in milk but some eat too much or too many salads and cause a condition in the stomach and the upper intestine which is painful.

Milk in its natural form taken from alfalfa or any of the grasses is quite healthful to the system. One requires naturally constituted dairy products on occasion which indicates cheese naturally aged. Protein can be derived from nuts and eggs with occasional meats. While protein is necessary for life or the rebuilding of your system, excessive protein in your system is the most common ailment today. The average person eats far too much protein for his own good. Excessive milk or protein in the diet causes chronic headaches and chronic sinus trouble, as you call it. Here again, imbalance causes these annoying symptoms. Another important food is honey. A teaspoon at each meal or a tablespoon once a day is desirable.

This may sound as though I am over simplifying but that is not true. The whole digestive program is simplicity but it is extremely essential to our program for the benefit of our loved ones. Do not fall into the trap of man made rules. Listen to your inner thoughts and change your diets instantly from day to day depending on your needs. If you have a reasonable amount of all the elements in the body at all times, you will have excellent health. Many deformities are merely caused by deficiency in the various chemical elements.

Now listen carefully . . . There is much discussion on artificial stimulants for your system or food elements. Avoid these strenuously, for most of these chemicals do find themselves in your system as a permanent food. These are generally designed to excite certain glands in your body which are known to create these chemicals within your system. They are not furnishing the necessary food elements; they are triggering your body into removing from the storehouses these elements, therefore, avoid any and all artificial devices for sooner or later you deplete your system of these chemical elements and you have done yourself much harm. Avoid any preservatives if possible. Avoid any stimulants, for any chemical element which you put into your body stimulates certain glands and will tend to cause an imbalance within your temple system. So be quite selective in your food intake. Maintain a normal level of vitamin intake along with minerals so that you vary your supplementary chemicals within the necessity of your moods and eat accordingly at that moment.

Another important subject we wish to talk about is your teeth. It is not known to man as yet but if one maintained a proper diet, contrary to what man feels is a fact today, he can grow and repair tooth structure. Decay is merely the lack of proper dietary environment for the teeth. If the gums are properly massaged with rough food, the vital blood and nerve fluid necessary for the growth and maintenance of the teeth will be supplied in sufficient quantities to maintain this enamel, as you call it. Since the body can replace bone structure within itself, does it not sound reasonable that the body also can replace bone structure in the teeth? This in probable and practical. If you have proper vitamin balance and roughage in your diet, tooth decay would be non-existent.

Most tooth pastes are more harmful to the teeth than beneficial. In order to get that beautiful luster, it seems to be in order. They put caustic agents in the paste to cleanse off the so-called plaque on your teeth. the very plaque that is put there by nature to protect your teeth, just to make a bright white smile. Take water and brush your teeth vigorously. Brush your gums towards the teeth. Take a pleasant mouthwash and rinse your teeth thoroughly then swish it around hard and you will find that you have a tingling, healthy mouth.

Chapter 33

The Nervous System

IN THE PREVIOUS chapter concerning diet, the functioning of the digestive system harmonics, for individual areas of your physical, dictate the selection of the material and a re-composition of material to replace spent cells in the system. This is a normal process.

You have a fluid nervous system which causes the thought patterns or harmonics to be transferred from the impulse center or the transfer center which we call the brain, to the areas of need. Your nervous system divides into just as fine, in fact finer, cells than your blood system. It is your nervous system that causes your re-generation of blood cells or the food derived from the blood cells to form tissue which harmonizes with adjacent tissue. Your body then is made up of many, many harmonics. Your thought patterns transmit themselves automatically to your nerve centers and are distributed to the point of necessity. You will be amazed to know that it is your nervous system which causes the reshaping of your physical, not you blood system. Your blood system is really a transferring device for food elements in your system. It is a transfer agent exclusively. If there is damage to the nervous system, it is normal that the damaged area will react to this impulse and send out harmonics which will overcome the condition automatically.

The fluid system within the nervous system is pure white in color and transparent. This may sound strange but it is true. We know that when one takes sedation in any manner, they take this sedation to numb the nervous system. Unfortunately, the same sedation which is administered to release the pain in a localized area also reacts to all other vital areas at the same time. This in turn, slows up the recuperative powers of the system and consequently disturbs the balance in the nervous system and in time sustains permanent damage. In some areas the nervous system withers and some organs cease to function with noticeable physical results. Therefore, any sedation you place in your system is dangerous to your system. I know what your medical science teaches, but you must break the pain cycle if you wish to be healed. So it behooves you to be more concerned over your nervous system than over your blood system.

Polio is the breaking down of the fluid in the nervous system. There are pockets of air and since there is not contact, continuous contact, through the fluid of the system, the area beyond this point does not circulate properly and the result is not what is to be desired. Each area of your nervous system has its own frequency. This has been duly recorded and it is known to man for they have devices now whereby they attach electrodes to the system at various points and record and confirm the proper functioning or malfunctioning of this particular transmittal force to the individual parts of the physical.

It behooves the individual to think harmoniously for when one injects a thought in their system, this thought, by their conscious mind or subconscious mind, activates and/or deactivates various functions of the physical. Your thought patterns are extremely essential to your well being for it is by your thought patterns that you have shaped your physical. A healthy attitude towards life is an expression used quite commonly in your phase of existence. What you think and what you observe when you see a happy person is they let you know that they are thinking along certain lines and their body reacts to their thoughts and they are healthy. I cannot emphasize strongly enough the necessity for a healthy attitude towards life. When one has a healthy attitude towards life, they take the conditions around and about them as they present themselves with an attitude of confidence. They are equal to the situation which they are confronted with. They attack their problems with confidence and enthusiasm and without fear.

You wonder about this disease you call cancer and you wonder why it happens. This is generally triggered by habits of thought; by deep emotional disturbances or frustrations. These frustrations are not harmonious with the normal harmonics of the physical being, and each thought is an avenue of expression and each thought reflects physically within the well being of the individual. So, if a person persists in holding a thought pattern which is non-consistent with their normal harmonics they create a harmonic in the system which develops an entity within itself because they are introducing a thought pattern which is contrary to their normal harmonics of life. In essence, this person is creating a battle between the healthy cells and the cells which are caught or generated or created by this thought. Your thoughts create the conditions; your thoughts alter the harmonics; your thoughts trigger your organs, so if you wish to reverse this process you have to eliminate the thought pattern that created the condition. That is why we say 'you are the complete master of your ship'. You create the image—no one else.

This is why we strongly advocate abstention from sedentary elements in your system. This is why these young people today burn up inside. It is because they are taking chemicals which upset the normal balance and the physical body is continually attempting to rid itself of these foreign elements. This is why many areas of the body, from time to time, tend to lose their mobility. The nervous system is the body builder or destroyer; the blood system merely feeds the body the elements which are needed to reconstruct the used cells. With the proper mental depression, one can will themselves into a complete sedentary condition and cause their own demise.

This may amaze you, but bread and sugar have more sedentary effect on the system, generally, than other music, for you are a series of symphonies. You call yourself to your demise. It behooves you, when you receive a blow on your physical, that you remain peaceful in your attitude and understand that if you allow this area to represent itself as it normally would with outside stimulus, that you would receive perfect restoration of the afflicted area. This is why we advise many patients to look and be true to yourself.

When you transmit the healing force, you overwhelm; you activate the nervous system not the blood system. In order to reinforce the nervous system, it is vital to have fish oils; unsaturated fats. Wheat germ and fish oil are essential to your well being. There is an element in the mollusk family which tends to destroy the nervous system. I highly recommend that you do not consume this food. Look to a new source of supplies which will give you your vitamins in a pure, natural condition.

Most people who eat a high protein diet generally neglect minerals and what you call vitamins in the system and consequently cause deficiency diseases. Within your physical being your blood system and your nervous system are interdependent with your thought patterns, anyone of which affects all. Be careful of your thinking, for you are creating a reaction whether it be favorable or unfavorable.

If you eat a balanced diet and relax, your body will extract from the food you consume, the elements that it needs to perpetuate itself. You could eat ten meals a day and lose weight or you could eat an improper diet and eat one meal a day and put on weight. Contrary to the theory of calorie counters, this is wrong. Your body will absorb from this food intake, the elements it requires for its needs and allow the excess materials to flow harmlessly through the digestive system and eliminate themselves. But if one does not receive the proper balance of food energy, the body retains this mass of material seeking to store it in hopes that it can extract natural food elements.

It is not how much you eat, but how well you eat that is important. That other element of well being which is important is muscle tone. Your muscles are formed by your thoughts. You can take any area on your body and give it the attention you wish and you find that this area of your physical reacts exactly to the stimulus of your thought. That is part of the maturing process in the physical body. Merely a change in thought pattern will react in physical fulfillment. You can change the shape of any area of your physical by thought control. I repeat—you can change ANY physical appearance or aspect of your body by controlled thought. You can think slender or you can think fat. That is why in witnessing the actions of an individual walking or talking, the motions of their hands, the way they stride, you can immediately know the manner of thought contained within this physical body. You telegraph your thought contained within this physical body. You telegraph your thought patterns to others by your physical manifestations of your thoughts. Any trained observer knows this. You are thought; you are the manifestation of thought. You are constantly creating and re-creating the image which you see in the mirror.

Your muscular tone is essential to your well being for your muscle tone controls the location and the relationship of your bone structure. Your muscles can dislocate various bone members and cause what you call pinched nerves. You can mentally, inadvertently, through steadfast thought patterns, dislocate various bones in your body. Each joint in your body, not just the vertebrae in your spine, has nerves passing through it and if there is a dislocation of muscle strain or muscle relationships, there is a dislocation of the relationship on the bones and consequently a pinched nerve results. This pinched nerve does not allow the full flow of energy to the affected areas beyond this point and consequently they suffer, not from malnutrition, but malfunctioning. for the signal is weak and so the activity of the nerve endings are reduced and you have a malfunction. The pain you feel in your various joints; the pain you feel when you have headaches is merely a pinched nerve area somewhere in our system caused by external force or internal force.

It is better when one has a headache or a pain, to localize this condition mentally by exploratory testing of the circuit throughout your system and locating the cause of the pinched nerve and relax these muscles or reverse the strain on these muscles and the headache will disappear. Taking sedation does not solve the problem. Sedation merely reduces the pain level and allows the condition to complicate itself and take hold or set. You can, at will, mentally locate the source and have assistance in relieving this condition or mentally cause it to rectify itself. Sedations are quite harmful to anyone's well being. Therefore, there is no excuse for the use of sedation since the individual has the ability to leave the physical body at any given time and come back to the physical at a controlled moment. One can readily allow their physical to re-harmonize itself under these conditions, for when the physical is allowed to function with out thoughts which disturb the balances within the system, it functions normally. THIS IS THE BASIS OF ALL HEALINGS.

When the individual who is to be healed has complete faith, they have dismissed, of that moment, all the negative thoughts which cause distress within their system. They have released all tensions of the nervous system as their muscle system reacts to their tensions. When they have relieved themselves of all thought patterns, their physical will automatically revert to the harmonious condition. In this way, the individual can heal himself. In sleeping soundly, one allows their physical to be free of all stress and strain and can recuperate or repair damage caused by anxiety and fear, which are the cause of the majority of all physical symptoms which you call disease. I wish to have you become completely aware of the fact that you have complete control of your physical. You are not the victim or external forces, you are the victim of erroneous thoughts. It behooves you to meditate daily and be quite conscious of your attitude towards your fellowman and life. Face each day with enthusiasm. Dismiss trepidation. This is the basic life control.

If one thinks with enthusiasm, one's physical expression can live indefinitely. You age only because of your thought patterns because you accept certain thought patterns of those around and about you. You say that you are expected to think certain ways at certain stages in your life and you forget muscle tone and consequently allow your physical to deteriorate. You, with the proper attitude, control the length of your sojourn on your plane of existence. There is no such thing as the aging process. There is a matter of deterioration of thinking reflected in the aging process.

Chapter 34

Proper Ingress

WE MADE A statement previously, that the aging process in a mental condition. There is no physical reason for a person to age if the individual would conduct himself according to the laws of the Great I Am. They would have a physical temple they could use indefinitely. It is a part of the process of life. If you would but reason, you would realize this is true.

Every cell in your temple renews itself daily. So, if one would eat the proper chemicals or food elements; rest at proper intervals; have a zest for life mentally; one could cause the function of the temple to right itself. When we speak of zest for life, we speak of anticipation of that which is ahead and that which is at hand, without fear.

It is very, very important that each individual cause himself to create physical exertion once or twice daily to the point of complete usage of all the muscles of the body. This causes the blood and nervous energy to circulate in every cell of the body to cleanse the toxins created by the re-generation process, to be removed from the localized areas that cause the flesh to become vital. You must breathe deeply, for the food for the brain and the food for digestion is the very air you breathe. You must exercise to the point where the lungs ache momentarily. Any exercise beyond this point is superfluous. Strenuous exercise can be just as dangerous as inactivity, for it depletes the body of it's normal balance of chemicals and secretions for proper functioning. Moderation is in order here.

The average person does not drink sufficient liquids to allow for chemical actions and reactions. For what causes your body to function is what you would call the oxidation or burning process. You chemically change food into it's basic elements and you distribute these basic elements, for they will be used by some activity to benefit the various organs and muscles in the body. Without the proper amounts of liquids, this becomes a sluggish procedure and various cell areas of your body are deprived of proper chemicals for their regeneration.

It is also necessary, upon consumption of the cells, that the waste matter or the ash of these cells, have completely oxidized and been carried away in the fluid system to be disposed of through your bladder, your bowel, or your sweat glands. It may be of interest to you as a side thought, that there are many, many people who are making money, as you call it, from surface chemicals which they spray on their persons or temples to neutralize the odor caused by the toxins secreted by their sweat glands.

If the individual ate the proper diet; had the proper liquid ingress, this condition would not exist. This condition is basically a condition whereby you have eaten too many fats; too many starches and your system and your kidneys and bladder are taxed to their capacity. They are not given sufficient liquid to allow this formation to distribute through many minute capillaries. When your bladder and kidneys are taxed, they over exert their capacity, then the avenue of the sweat glands enfold into a rhythm of relief. That is why some have sweaty feet and some have a line across the base of their skull where they sweat and it goes down their neck and down their back and also sweat across their chest and in their arm pits. This is normal.

Normally. when one has sufficient liquid in their system to flush the toxins through, you will only have water in your sweat glands. Consequently, un-rendered fats or starches will be present to create odor. All these simple deodorant chemicals do, is to neutralize the odor the same as you would spray a garbage can. We are not attempting to be overly facetious in our discussion but we wish to have it clearly understood concerning the functions spiritually and emotionally and physically as far as your temple is concerned.

In order to express ourselves in a simple way, to be readily understood by all who read these words, we may get technical on occasion but we will try to remain as simple as possible and also practical.

One requires oil in their system; un-rendered oil. If one must eat meat, one must bake it at a low temperature so as not to render the fats. We do not care whether you are speaking of meat as fish or fowl or animal; when you render the fat, it is indigestible and merely clogs up the digestive tract. That is all it does. It goes through the system and actually prevents, on many occasions, elements which are nutritional in value, from being absorbed into the system. It forms a fatty coating in your cell structures as well as in your blood stream, as you call it, and these prevent proper function of the system. So, we advise strongly that you eat a minimum amount of meat or in the process of eating it you will destroy elements which are highly beneficial to your body.

If you use heat beyond the normal temperature of the sun you are destroying the basic elements which are beneficial to your body. You can accomplish the same effect by causing a vacuum to replace boiling food. You merely boil meat, vegetables and other elements to break up the cellular structure so it is easier to chew. When you lower the air pressure, you effectively cause the liquids in the cellular structure of that which you are cooking to explode and break up the cellular structure the same as heat. Heat expands and causes heated moisture to expand and explode to break down the cellular structure. As far as breaking down the cellular structure is concerned, it does not matter which way you choose to do it, but it makes a tremendous difference in the nutritional value of that which you have either destroyed by cooking, or preserved with vacuum which does not destroy any of the nutritional value of the food. This is known as vacuum cooking.

With cooking food, you destroy it's delicate taste. The taste of these fruits and vegetables are lost in the process. I think the most dramatic vegetable of all is the pea. Eat a raw pea and it is delicious. Cook the same pea and it is mush. Carrots are delicious raw, break them down and soften them up with vacuum and they are very palatable.

Your vitamins which are essential to your system and your minerals which are essential to your system are all in these fruits and vegetables and grains. It is not necessary to eat flesh to maintain the equilibrium of both vitamins and minerals; the equilibrium of perpetual renewal of your temple.

Herbs are the natural sources of what you would call medicinal value. If these were included in the diet on a regular basis there would be no illness of physical sources. Most illness, as you understand it, is brought about by emotional distress and improper ingress of the food elements required for the proper rebuilding process of your temples. There are no plants placed in your realm of influence which are what you call weeds. Every plant has its purpose. Everyone should have available to them, all the herbs and make it a habit of drying these leaves and sprinkling these dried leaves on the various items which they prepare for eating. If you had a right combination of herbs, you would be beyond or immune to influenza; the common cold and illnesses of this nature. There are chemicals in these extractions which tone the body to such an extent that the aging process would be non-existent. The common dandelion, if consumed at regular intervals, along with other herbs, would eliminate what you call the common cold. Burdock and thistle will eliminate what you call the influenza condition. The allergies would also disappear.

Herbs are as essential as the water you drink. Make it a point to find a source for these; it will be beneficial. Heart trouble would be non-existent if one understood that the herb such as the mint family is essential to good health. The chemicals contained in your medicines are all contained in the herb family. Onions, garlic and parsley are all essential herbs.

We do not believe in fasting. There is a reasoning by man, that if he spends a day strictly on a liquid diet, this is a step in the right direction. It merely flushes out many of the toxins from the system. It helps rid the body of any excess amount of toxins but if the ingress was proper, this would not be required. And meanwhile, while you are fasting, you are not feeding yourselves, but you are constantly in the process of rebuilding the proper chemical elements for the proper rebuilding process and you need the food to do this. You are doing damage by fasting. You are not accomplishing that which you wish to accomplish.

Now, if you desire to have the proper weight, you must investigate your intake of the vital elements and when you have the proper balance; the intake of proper elements and you are in a relaxed state of being, your weight will become normal automatically. This is a vast subject. We have touched on the basics to give you more factual documentaries of our point of view; information you can work with to give you the secret of eternal life physically as well as spiritually.

There are a few other points we wish to discuss with you. The early law which is accredited to Judaism; that you do no eat two proteins at the same time, is as valid today as it was in our day. You have triggering devices in your throat in conjunction with your saliva ducts, which determine which combinations of which excretions to place in your system, depending on which protein you are chewing at the time, so that when you eat a protein, your body will digest this certain protein separately. You may eat this protein separately and place the proper digestive in your system to digest this one and then at the same meal, singularly eat another protein and your body will send a different combination of excretions into your system and you will digest this properly. The Jewish Law says so. We know this is probable. It would be better if you did confine your meals to one protein at a time. If you eat proteins in combination such as meat and cheese at the same meal, your system becomes confused and that which is placed in your system is improper for digestion and you will have an uncomfortable feeling in your stomach. This I can assure you; you will have a bloating feeling in your stomach.

Broiled foods, of necessity, must be avoided. Fried foods must positively be avoided, for these rendered fats are not only indigestible but these are the fats that your body does not have mechanisms to digest. You will find people who have swollen joints, hardening of the arteries and diseases of this order, are victims of their eating habits and you will find that they have eaten many fried or broiled foods in their lifetime. Call it arthritic conditions if you wish but it is just an accumulation of indigestible matter in the joints due to circulation problems and undigested foods. People ruin their kidneys in this manner. Milk is in the same category. Natural cheeses are quite desirable. Processed cheeses are to be avoided.

You want roughage in your system? Many people mistakenly eat an over abundance of lettuce, endives and leaves of this nature figuring they are receiving roughage in their diet. This is true but the average person does not chew their salads as thoroughly as they might and cause masses which do not digest in the system.

Your body is built to normally eat the fruits of the vine; the fruits of the trees and roots from the earth. You are not normally meat eating animals. The more flesh one eats—I'm not speaking of fish as flesh—the more materialistic one becomes in nature. You must realize that the meat eating habits of the nation are in disproportion to what they should be. Man is eating three times the flesh he needs. A meal should be 60% to 70% fruits and vegetables and the remainder in flesh, fish or fowl. If one would maintain this percentage, one would find himself in excellent health.

Chapter 35

Emotional Conduct

WE WOULD LIKE to speak on emotional conduct and it's relationship to one's well being. Emotions have more to do with the metabolism of the body than any single element of control of the system. Each of your glands is controlled by your emotions.

Consequently, your thought patterns control the amount of excretions of the various organs into your system. When you are contented and relaxed, your body functions normally but when you become distressed, you cause certain organs to function abnormally and this causes an imbalance of fluids in your system and causes a faulty metabolism. If this emotional strain is maintained for any particular length of time, this abnormality will persist and you will have depleted certain organs or glands of their excretions and cause what you know of as deficiency diseases.

Doctors are just realizing that this is a field of medicine which they have not been seriously concerned with for many, many years. They are just beginning to realize that this is basic in medicine. This is a cause and affect phase of medicine that is basically psychology with a complete understanding of the relationship of emotions and glandular disturbances, is the basis of ALL medicine. They have been concentrating for hundreds and hundreds of years on alleviating symptoms of the end result of the conditions caused by emotional imbalance. They have not scientifically indulged in experimentations to the point where they can specifically state that certain emotional conditions trigger certain emotional reactions and physical responses so that they can document the effects of emotions on your glandular system. We are putting pressure to bear on the medical profession in an endeavor to cause them to become inspired to delve into this essential phase of medicine.

They are backing into this essential phase of medical research. All we are saying is, once they establish the relationship between the hormone imbalance as a triggering emotional fact, then we will be able to determine the depletion of the various hormone building vitamins, minerals, and oils in the system. And we will be able to determine which supplements to give the individual on a limited basis, to cause these organs that become depleted, to be restored to their normalcy. But here again this intake of abnormal hormones should be limited to the extent of creating a temporary correction, for we must correct the cause, which is imperfect thinking on the part of the individual.

There are those who persistently think in error for years on end and they create so called diseases which are terminal in nature. When they correct their thinking, their body will respond to the corrected thinking and the body will automatically . . . remember this carefully . . . the body will AUTOMATICALLY repair the conditions and render the protective devices and rebuilding devices to bring itself back to normal without the aid of medical science.

If one is careful to examine oneself, examine their thought process, one can determine the disturbing elements and correct them with a corresponding correction in the physical. Your physical being is as sensitive to your thought as you are to music. Music creates a mood in your being. Music has great healing power if you allow yourself to be deeply engrossed in its quality. There again you must find the music the nature of which causes you to lose yourself completely into its structure. Once you find the music which causes you to lose yourself completely, it would be well for you to listen to this music intently for an hour or an hour and a half each day. This will be food for your being. You may have other activities which you will transact while intently listening but it's therapeutic value is beyond your present comprehension.

I do not know what they are going to call this new phase of medicine but this is the modern basic concept of medicine. It will require more training by the doctor but it will be rewarding. You can gain or lose weight at will. You can gain or lose vitality at will, depending upon the emotional stresses or lack of stresses in the situations you find yourself in. Man knows now, some of the dramatic reactions to emotional disturbances on the physical. There are those who are continually disturbed, distressed by those around and about them, due to frustration which is a mild form of anger, and they secrete an abnormal amount of acid into their digestive system and create ulcers, cancer of the stomach and diseases of that nature.

We also know those who have deep rooted fears of acceptance by their fellowman will cause abnormal pressures on the heart muscles and actually create what you call heart attacks. Many, many heart attacks are caused by emotional restrictions.

We talk about diseases of the colon. These are directly related to emotion. These too are triggered by fear and anxiety. Fear and anxiety and frustration are other culprits which the individual must overcome. You can allow fear and anxiety to consume you or you can consume it. It is encouraging to know that once one overcomes fear and anxiety, their body responds almost instantaneously to normalcy. It takes a certain amount of time, a matter of days, to reactivate the cells which were damaged by the abnormal excretions of the hormones, enzymes and other elements of body building and digestion, but the time element is relatively short.

So one must learn to live at peace with themselves to overcome illness, as you call it. One must not fear; one must live in anticipation and one must learn to accept the conditions that they find around and about them, knowing full well that they can cope with any condition they find themselves involved in.

There are doctors who are seriously considering this new medicine but have not openly declared their position. There are many who are aware of this but have no means of documentation so they practice it quietly and abstrusely, but it must and will come to the surface and we will make every effort that causes it to have the proper place and proper dignity in medicine, for this is proper medicine. Emotions and food element intake are strongly inter related and must be documented for the benefit of all mankind.

Chapter 36

Exercise

It is essential, as we stated before, to exercise every muscle in your body at least once a day. When we speak of peace and serenity, we do not necessarily mean the individual attains a restful state of being. This is in error. If you could find an exercise form where you could lose yourself completely and the exercises were for a few brief moments where you forget the body as such and become deeply engrossed in the activity, this would be a perfect state of serenity. When you reach the state where the blood rushes through your veins and your nerve fluid rushes through the sheaves without mental exertion or deviation, then you have attained serenity and peace.

Here are some basic exercises which you could do while sitting, reclining or laying flat. We would prefer that each student meditate in a reclining position. We prefer that each student, prior to meditation, exercise each leg, separately strained against the arms, then both legs jointly strained against the arms, then each leg stretched to the air, toes pointed up, singularly and jointly with hands parallel to the body, palms flat to the mat.

Another exercise is both hands locked behind the head pushing against the head with the head resisting the movement. Then pull one foot, pressing against the knee while the other foot is pressing against the knee, resisting in each case. Then the fist of one hand in the opposing hand, laying on the abdominal area, hands resisting each other then reversing the procedure. Then across the chest, elbows out, keeping the fingers pulling one against the other, reverse the grip; repeat. This should be done each time before you meditate.

It is also important that you breathe slowly and deeply, expanding your lungs fully to the count of six (6). Then you will slowly and rhythmically, exhale this air to the count of 6 until your lungs are completely evacuated. Hold this evacuation condition for the count of 6. Repeat 6 times. Then you will enter into the prayerful mood needed to receive our wisdom through meditation.

You will find that these exercises will have used every muscle combination in your body and will have relaxed you completely. These should be repeated at least once a day. Now, if it is inconvenient for you to be in a reclining position you will find that you can do this sitting in a chair. It will not be that different. When you are through with your exercises and breathing, place your bodies in a state of limbo so that you can forget that you have a physical being. So that you are not limited by your awareness of your physical body and can release yourself from the limitations one places on their physical being and expand oneself to the higher realm which is available to all.

Each person is part of the whole. Each person is a part of the Great I Am. So, each and everyone is of equal value to the Master.

Do not shirk these exercises. You will find that they will advance the individual far more readily than just sitting. For when one merely sits and breathes, one has not relaxed their being. their physical being, so that they can loose awareness of self. That is why, on many occasions, it is difficult for individuals to transcend their limitations.

When you walk, walk vigorously. It is not necessary to jog for your health. More people injure themselves by jogging because it is beyond the normal capacity of the body to recuperate. Remember, relaxation is being engrossed completely in a form of activity and being unconscious of self, whether it be tennis or tiddly-winks. It is the placement of oneself in a position where you lose awareness of self and become completely engrossed in an activity which is constructive. Even becoming engrossed in pulling weeds is far more useful than in running two miles. It is the combination of mental attitude and physical relationship to that attitude which is important not the activity itself or the mental attitude in itself, it is the combination of the two. Relaxation is a total activity, not resting and lazing around. Inactivity is one of the worst conditions you can create for good health. You must begin the habit of being active in one way or another AT ALL TIMES.

Chapter 37

The Balance of Elements

You MUST UNDERSTAND that our life is affected by the relative movement of the elements around the sphere you call the world. Since all activity generates electricity, it is not surprising to find the mere fact of water evaporating from the sphere should accumulate and condense. In the process of accumulation, electrical charges are built up and in order to maintain a balance, there is a discharge of electricity back to the earth plane from time to time, to affect a norm in the electrical field in which you live.

That is why it is difficult for us to penetrate or come through to you, as you call it, during an electrical storm, as you refer to it, because the electrical field of this discharge is like a wall to you and your material plane. The only reason you have lightening storms is that in certain periods the evaporation process is concentrated and that is the abnormal balance of power between the earth and the surrounding atmosphere. It is a means of equalization or normalization of the electrical field surrounding your earth body.

You are all living within this magnetic field. This is a shield which enables life to exist. If plant life or animal life were to be exposed to the great forces from outer space, they would disintegrate and disperse, for the force would be too great. This is understandable if one realizes that if one were to fertilize a field in moderation, the field would flourish. If someone were to take the same fertilization compound and concentrate it beyond the normal absorption rate of the living matter, you would find that life would disintegrate also. So, moderation is extremely important. Balance of elements is extremely important for all existence. Consequently, if on the lower plane, you haven't the balance of food intake in your system, you create imbalance in electrical energies in your system or abnormality of the function of various organs plus causing internal explosions within your system and you call this illness.

Your environment is important to your health. One must live in rural areas so one can absorb the pure chemicals in the air as you breathe. There must be a concerted effort on the part of mankind in general, to plant green grasses, bushes and trees, for they generate the moisture which moistens the soil and allows the air to obtain the chemicals it needs. In the process of raining, heavy dews separate these impurities in the air and cause them to be driven into the soil so they can be separated into the proper elements and purified for future use. It is because they cleared the land in the deserts that there are deserts. There is a plane where scraggly vegetation can no longer support the soil; thus a desert is formed.

The same devices affect spiritual growth. For when one plants a thought, it grows as a tree grows. It branches out and services many.

When one fails to create fruitful thoughts, it becomes a pattern of self indulgence and thoughtlessness and you create a desert surrounding your soul. This is serious, but many do it. Many people who are lonely do this. They send out these negative thoughts and they reap the winds of the desert. We constantly nourish that which is around and about us to be nourished, fruitful or otherwise.

Also, there must be a balance in your food intake. You can take too much nourishing food or certain elements and do just as much damage as a deficiency of the same food element. Your body discharges that which it does not require, but you must understand that it is the activity within the body which will determine which elements it will discharge as surplus. So, some phase of your being, in the process of discharging excessive elements, must be depleted because of that normal activity. Consequently, this also results in deficiency activity. Moderation is the word; balance is the word. Ultimately, you will find that you will sense within yourself, the food elements you require to maintain normalcy.

Diseases of all body functions are causes by abnormalities of food intake. But here again, your metabolism is not only a function of maintaining a normal balance of elements in your system, but it is affected by your emotional condition at any given time. Your emotions will change your balance requirements from time to time. When you are under deep stress, you build up certain elements faster than others in your body to a point of major imbalance. So, your metabolism varies form hour to hour, day to day, week to week. But there is a norm which is maintained when you are in a meditative state. That is the secret of longevity and being devoid of what you call illness.

Meditating methodically and regularly is quite desirable. It is desirable at times for the individual to take food supplements, for in this day and age, a man's foolishness and his laziness, renders most of the food he prepares for his consumption, impotent. Supplements of natural elements, as the body would normally consume it, are important. Do not be fooled by artificial stimulants which supposedly give the same chemical affects, for there is more than chemical relationships and elements to bring about the consumption and transferal of energy from one form to useful energy for your being. So do not second guess nature, as you call it, for Mother Nature is not fooled. She may smile or frown at your wisdom or ignorance of her laws but she will prevail. She will always prevail, if you turn yourself over to her, re-establish your balance in your system for proper sustaining of life.

Live with your hunches. There are certain times when you have urges to eat certain food elements excessively. Do not consider this abnormal. Consider this urge to be normal, for this is a way of telling you that you have deprived yourself of a balance which is essential to your system and you are using this device to re-establish balance within your system.

You must learn that when you have the proper balance of elements required by your physical allotted to you each day, your body will absorb that which is required and dispose of all others, including foreign elements now residing in your physical. In other words, what we are saying, is that when you have an internal consumption of all the required elements, each and every day, your body will assume a normal slender physical appearance, The retained liquids, ashes, and foreign substances which put on weight will no longer exist. You will extend your life span by years and years in this manner.

Stay away from sedation or foods which are sedation oriented, for they disrupt the nervous system. There is no need to drink other than water, juices, fruit of the vine, fruit of the grain and fruit of the tree. Cultivate eating habits which are healthy. Consume unsaturated fat oils. They are essential to your well being. Fish oils are useful to your well being also. When they are extracted at normal temperatures, rendered fats are highly indigestible. The great American Tragedy is a char-broiled hamburger, steak and what you call hot dogs, for they all render the fats and cause indigestion.

Chapter 38

Longevity

EXERCISE, DIET AND meditation are all important to longevity. Your spiritual food, as you know by now, is harmonious vibration. This is important, for this is the food for your spiritual being; this is the food your spiritual being builds upon and is derived from; various noises, vibrations and music around and about you.

It is necessary for one to cause themselves to be in what you call a prayerful attitude in order to be nourished by the higher vibrations of our plane of existence. Food for the spiritual being or food for your soul is constantly being changed, renewed and rejected. Each individual with whom you make contact emits excess vibration. When you are in the vicinity of another individual, you radiate vibrations and they radiate vibrations and these vibrations either mingle together in harmony or are repelled. This is why you are attracted to certain personalities and become uneasy with others for, each has his own peculiar harmonious being. Those who wish to proceed to a higher realm of accomplishment, therefore, must be especially careful to associate with those whose vibrations are in an advanced state, for they then will absorb this food. This food is growth food.

Now you have the proper attitude and you have eaten the proper chemical elements but the third phase is just as important as the other two, for unless you relax and exercise properly, you do not circulate these chemicals through your system. To prove this point, you could disintegrate your flesh person by merely having a specific pattern of harmonics and you could disintegrate any object or individual, so each and everyone must have a period of relaxation daily. Each one must have a period of meditation daily. The relaxation circulates the spiritual food and the physical exercise circulates the material food. It was stated in one of the previous lectures, that there have been those in the past who have remained on your planet four, five and six hundred years, by your standards. This is a fact. Therefore, maintain a balance and you will maintain your physical to an infinite level.

We insist that if one would learn to meditate; one must first place their physical in a sub-level concern. Look to a complete absence of awareness of your physical being and dismiss egotistical emotions. This is the only state in which we can contact you. There are those who become anxious. They feel as though they must concentrate their thought in a controlled area. This is what you call the door which opens or closes the avenue of expression through which we communicate. Unless one becomes alert to the great forces and opens themselves to us one will not succeed. When the disciple Paul said, 'I die daily', he merely said that he concentrates daily.

Each of you, as an individual, once you have purified yourself, can conjure up, if you wish to use this phrase, a great multiplication of a particular force to overwhelm those around and about you. It will only multiply on the strength of the motive of the source of the energy. That is why, and you may wonder and you may have wondered in the past, when Jesus walked amongst the multitudes He would say 'rise up and follow me' and the individual did not hesitate to rise and follow, for he saw the vibration which was required for the whole. There are twelve basic vibratory forces and when you have the proper balance of all twelve, you have a focusing power which is of the same category as that which fed through Jesus. He relied heavily on the strength not of the individuals, but of the combined vibratory plane of all. I hope this is clear. It is rather difficult for people to overcome the tendency of being self contained. This will enable you to record wisdom which has not been given to the common man through these sessions. (Spirit is speaking about the information in this book.) The information for this book was given by Spirit through Rev. Wagner using the combined energies of the group of people meditating together for the sole purpose of receiving this material for this book. It took the energies of all in the group to receive this information.

The aging process, as I stated in a previous lecture, is brought about by the imbalance of these three elements of life. You must remember when you see a youth you see apparent unbound energy and you have said to yourself either audibly or mentally; 'I wish I had that energy again.' Note the energy of youth, the enthusiasm of youth, the imagination of youth, the complete relaxation of youth. Youth listens, youth plays, youth is serious, youth is mindful of being able to cooperate with other youths, they are attracted to other youth for here is the secret of life. You are careful to give them an afternoon nap. You are careful what food you feed a child and the exercise they receive distributes this food and energy properly. What I am saying, is that exercise, proper nutrition and proper emotional attainment are of equal importance to the individual in maintaining the spiritual and physical condition of a basis where we may communicate directly with mankind.

A child does not play with imaginary beings. A child is playing with reality. He sees what you call the supernatural and he accepts it as being common. It is only the aged who say this is imagination; these things do not exist and this causes the child to change his mode of thinking. You tell a Young lady—'when you are physically a certain age you must quiet down; you must act in a certain manner.' You have then set up the conventions which bring about your aging.

Certain types of thoughts deplete certain of your harmonics so you must feed your soul and feed your body and distribute this food (thoughts) on a day to day basis. Aging is not an inevitable factor of life. It is only man's figment of imagination or man's standard. It is a device conjured up by man. It is an escape from the trials of his daily schooling. Man is inherently lazy and tends to activity when he is forced. There are those among you who need no pressure to accomplish their missions, but they are few and far between. The average individual is involved in self indulgence and apathy.

When Jesus spoke of sin, He spoke of the elements which tend to the destruction of the individual and the forces. This is sin. For these are the emotions or the lack of emotions which bring about the aging process. If you want to rejuvenate yourself or renew yourself or maintain a level of existence, you must have enthusiasm. You must have a purpose which overwhelms the individual so that one does not become at a state of existence whereby awareness of self is equal to the awareness of the force or the mission. When the two are equal, that is a point of de-generation or the aging process, for you lack enthusiasm and you lack purpose. You start leaning on the oars, as you say, and you let others row the boat.

Do this often enough and you can age rapidly, for aging is a state of mind. If you are careful of the intake of music and sound; if you are careful of the chemical elements required for your physical being and balance all with a proper approach mentally and emotionally, there is no death. You could maintain this physical being indefinitely if you conduct yourself in a balance of emotion. I repeat—YOU COULD MAINTAIN THIS PHYSICAL BEING INDEFINITELY IF YOU CONDUCT YOURSELF IN A BALANCE OF EMOTION, AWARENESS OF SPIRITUAL FOOD AND AWARENESS OF MATERIAL FOOD. Every sound which you expose yourself to is food, either constructive or destructive. You now know the secret of eternal life. Cherish it for there is no substitute for purpose and enthusiasm.

You may have wondered at times why children scream and holler and make noise. They are emitting life; they are absorbing life and they play with each other with enthusiasm. They distribute life amongst each other; they imagine with purpose and they grow; they grow on their purpose. These are the guides; these are the forces which control your physical and spiritual being. Guard these well; cultivate these well and you will live eternal life.

May the Great I Am cause your lights to be clear; cause your desires to be pure and cause you to relax in the knowledge that you are part of the Great I Am who is ever desirous of caring for all that are part of this Great I Am. Do not live in fear, for fear shuts the door. Relax in the blessed light and the Great I Am and your life will be as you would have it.

Chapter 39

Summary

WE WILL CONCLUDE by merely reminding you that it is extremely important to your well being that you choose your associates and mates well. It is through your association with other individuals that your frustrations and expectations and general well being are determined.

Each of you is spiritually clean or clear when you are born, but through association, you absorb a certain amount of the magnetic field of those around and about you. It is also true that you can be depleted of your energy by association. Those around and about you who are of lesser advancement will naturally absorb energies from your being and as they absorb at a greater rate than you can reabsorb from the God-head, you can become exhausted spiritually.

It is true you must give of yourself to advance, There is no deviation what so ever from this. You advance by giving of yourself and that which you give will be of the past and allows you to absorb from the God-head, the present and future. This may be creating selfish motivation in many people. It may give some people an incentive to give for a change rather than absorb, but regardless of the immediate motivation, the fact remains that one must give to advance in their development.

We are continually aware of your motivating force and we control the type of energy; type of food which you dispose of for the benefit of those around and about you. We must reemphasize the fact that your motivation or your reason for expanding energy is an extremely important factor in your advancement. Sometimes we know full well that your goals and incentives are incorrect. We will attempt to put obstacles in your paths to keep you from pursuing these wrong directions but if you ignore them we will feed you as you demand. Those of you who choose the path of non-ego love, will receive the love, the fulfillment, the blessings of good works that all mankind desires. We will feed you as you demand. The love force, the hate force are available to all individuals upon their demand. You seek and you will find that which you seek. The motive is a key to your progress and the motive alone is the key. There are no magic words, no gifted ones; only those who wish to extend themselves are the so-called gifted ones.

We cannot stress this too much for this and this alone is the key to your expansion, the key to your unfolding; the key to your ability to tap this great force and expand on it many times. For we immediately replenish in the exact proportion to that energy which is expended. Sometimes, we restore those who have changed the course; who have depleted their energies and then through revelation, recognize the futility of their selfish motives and become unselfish and we are capable of expanding individuals a thousand fold.

You control the food which nourishes your soul; you alone; for you are the motivating force. You control the conditions; we fulfill the demands for your motivations in proportion to that which pleases the God-head. This is only encouraging to those who want to ascend to find themselves on the right path. For you excel on an ever increasing plane of travel. You travel, not in what you call a straight line graph, but an ever increasing graph when you strike the right motive. Any one and everyone has the capability, without exception to attain this element of advancement.

May the Great I Am further excel in your advancement with this great love force and may you overcome fear and doubt and be whole in the eyes of your Father, the Great I Am. So be it.

Glossary

Aura—a fluxing combination of color seen around one's body. It is a way for spirit to read your thoughts; each train of thought produces a different color.

Crime—a result of sin. Any serious wrong doing; An action that is deemed injurious to the public.

Disease—dis-ease within the body usually caused by wrong thinking.

Force—used in this instance; the force you attract or trigger by your intense desire to use this force for the benefit of those around and about you.

Higher Realm—the spiritual realm—the place you are capable of contacting through prayer, thought and meditation and can communicate with God.

Healing Force—the force used by the laying on of hands and prayer to re—harmonize or to bring the body back into harmony.

Illness—a dis-harmony in the body caused by the habit of an erroneous conception of yourself and your relationship with those around and about you.

Meditation—quiet supplication—listening for God's love and direction.

Melchizedek—high priest to God as referenced in the Bible; Genesis 14:18 also a member of the White Brotherhood.

Physical Body—a manifestation of the mental image created by the individual to carry out one's mission on the earth plane.

Prayer—supplication from the heart. Talking or communicating with God

Sin—in this instance—being born with the lack of knowledge of what is real and what isn't. Being ignorant of God's law's.

Spirit—the animating principal of life; a vital essence. God is spirit; you, the real you is also spirit. that is how we communicate with God and He us.

Spiritual Body—each person is part of the spiritual body; part of the great force.

Spiritual Force—the animating principle of life; the vital essence to influence, affect or control; the force of circumstances combined for action.

Thought—the product of mental activity; the motivating thought or prayer, depending on the intensity of your desire, determining the level of contact with the Higher Realm or Spirit World.